Contents

Owd Lancashire

Lancashire is a county in the north-west of England, known predominantly as a region for cotton textile manufacturing and located on the Irish Sea. The county borders were reduced considerably in the 1970s following numerous boundary changes, including the loss of Furness to Cumbria as well as Manchester, Merseyside and Cheshire.

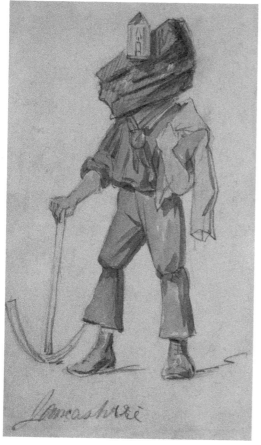

John Leech nineteenth-century caricature of the county of Lancashire.

Lancashire's
Food and Drink

Emma Kay

AMBERLEY

First published 2020

Amberley Publishing
The Hill, Stroud, Gloucestershire, GL5 4EP
www.amberley-books.com

Copyright © Emma Kay, 2020

The right of Emma Kay to be identified as the
Author of this work has been asserted in accordance
with the Copyrights, Designs and Patents Act 1988.

ISBN 978 1 4456 9565 5 (print)
ISBN 978 1 4456 9566 2 (ebook)

British Library Cataloguing in Publication Data.
A catalogue record for this book is available from
the British Library.

Typesetting by SJmagic DESIGN SERVICES, India.
Printed in Great Britain.

TRADITIONS AND FESTIVALS

In some regions of Lancashire, most notably Bowland on a Good Friday, the day was named 'Cracklin' Friday'.

The Forest of Bowland was once a huge hunting ground with its own forest courts where grouse, wild boar, deer and wolves roamed. Children would go house to house with a small basket and beg for cracknels – small wheat cakes like Passover bread, but shorter and made with butter or lard.[1] Cracknels are as old as medieval times and appear in numerous recipe books. They were hard, brittle baked cakes or biscuits. Fig or fag pies were traditionally eaten in Lancashire on Mid-Lent Sunday and were sometimes referred to as quick-step pudding. However, these were also popular in other regions of the North including Nottinghamshire and Derbyshire. One pie that consists largely of onions, potatoes and sometimes cheese is often linked specifically to the county. Butter, Catholic or Friday pie has its origins in the Catholic community and the abstinence of meat on a Friday. It was also known as air pie in the Bolton area.[2] Traditionally served with red cabbage, it is thought to have established itself in Preston, amongst the growing swell of Irish Catholic migrants to the town in the nineteenth century. However, I have found evidence of this dish dating much further back, to at least the seventeenth century, when it appears in Hannah Woolley's 1670 book of household management.[3]

A Friday Pie without Fish or Flesh

Wash a good quantity of green Beets, and pluck out the middle string, then chop them small; with two or three ripe Apples well relished, season it with Pepper,

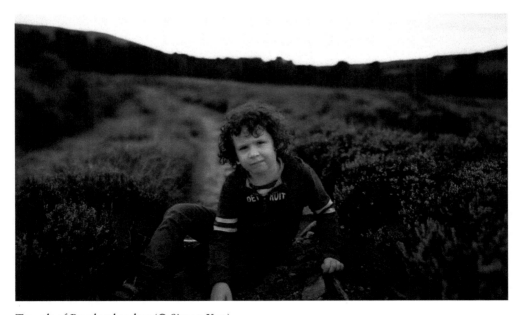

Trough of Bowland today. (© Simon Kay)

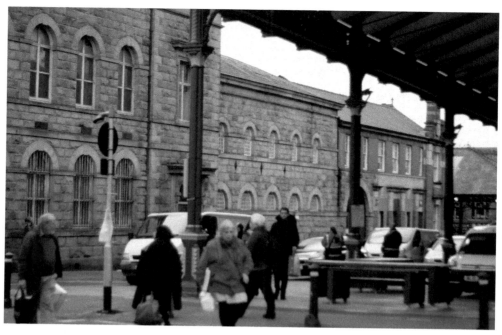

Preston. (© Nick Kay)

Salt and Ginger, then add to it some Currans, and having your Pie ready, and Butter in the bottom, put in these herbs, and with them a little Sugar, then put Butter on the top, and close it and bake it, then cut it up, and put in the Juice of a Limon and Sugar.

Tosset cakes are associated with Stalmine near Poulton-le-Fylde and could be a corruption of St Oswald. They are very similar to other village fair/feast/club cakes including Goosnargh cakes, Garstang Fair cakes and Pilling cakes. Each village vied with the other to make the best creations. Incidentally, Goosnargh, at least since the Victorian period and possibly earlier, is also renowned for both its duck and chicken, cooked in the kitchens of many reputable restaurants and pubs throughout Britain.

Stalmine village used to celebrate an event called the Tosset Feast, with numerous activities like wrestling and races and everyone indulging in tosset cakes. This was centred around the church in Stalmine, a church dedicated to St Oswald. St Oswald's Feast would have been better known as T'Oswald Feast, or Tosset! Bevan Ridehalgh from the *Lancashire Magazine* passed on her recipe to Glyn Hughes to include in his book *The Lost Foods of England*.

Tosset Cakes

1lb plain flour
1lb butter
4oz caster sugar

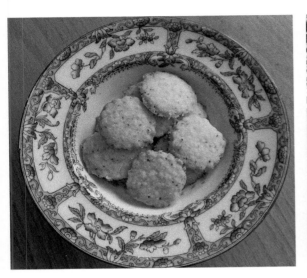

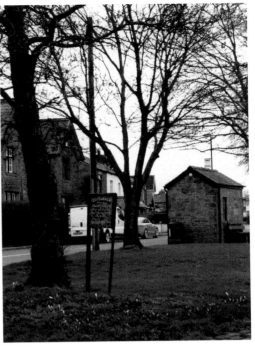

Above: Tosset cakes. (© Emma Kay)

Right: Goosnargh village green. (© Nick Kay)

1 teaspoon caraway seeds, 1 teaspoon coriander seeds (crushed)

Sieve flour and sugar into a bowl, rub in the butter and the seeds and mix well to form a smooth dough. Leave the dough in a cool place overnight. Then roll this out to about ¼ inch thick. Using a cutter or glass, cut out rounds of about 2 inches in diameter. Place these on a floured baking board and sprinkle with caster sugar. Bake in a preheated oven at 350 degrees f/180 degrees Celsius Gas mark 4. Do not allow them to brown; they are baked when just firm to the touch – which should take 15 to 20 minutes. Allow them to cool and then thickly cover them with icing sugar.[4]

Pace-egging (or messing around) is an ancient Lancashire custom of colouring and decorating eggs at Easter time. Pace-eggers, or 'jolly boys', took the form of mummers including a mix of men and young boys dressed in character as a hunchback, a long-nosed man and a prisoner who sang the ballad 'The Ouldest Man at Tea' while performing a short dramatic piece which included a policeman and a judge. The character of 'Owd nan' or 'Miss Kitty' (a man in a veil) carried a basket and they all moved from house to house in procession through the village streets. One traditional ballad from these theatrics titled 'Beg Your Leave' was collected by Annie Gilchrist at Overton Village in 1906. It goes as follows:

I'll beg your leave fine kind gentlemen and ladies of re-nown, if you'll please to make us room … we will sing to you a song, …You please to make us room, we will sing to you a song, And we'll call in our comerades and call them one by one. So we're jolly

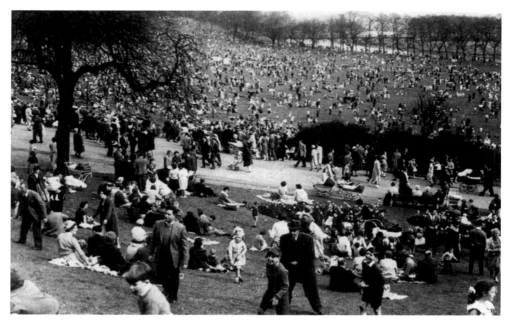

Pace-eggers at Avenham Park, Preston, 1956. (Courtesy of Preston Digital Archive)

boys, … we do no harm…Wherever we do go, For we've come the pace-egg-ing, As you very well do know… So the first that does come in, He is a blooming youth, he courts all the pretty girls, and always tells them truth; He says he never deceives them, but is always kind and true.

And 'tis his delight both day and night in drinking of strong wine. [brew]…[5]

From the turn of the twentieth century, pace-egging in the county became more about the art of rolling eggs down the hill. In Avenham Park, Preston, huge gatherings took place on Easter Monday to do just that, a tradition which continues today.

Tharff, or tharf/thor/thar cake was a coarse oatmeal and treacle cake. It derives from the Old English term *tharf*, meaning need or necessity.[6] So, perhaps it was cake designed to meet a basic need. It was a lot like a flat parkin apparently eaten on 5 November, a date that coincides with an old feast in honour of Thor. In John Trotter Brockett's *A Glossary of Northern Country Words*, he explains that they were rolled out very thinly and might also consist of rye and barley. They were often hung up in large quantities, with a pole that ran through the centre for storage.[7] This cake is often attributed to Derbyshire and Yorkshire, but in older works it is nearly always connected to Lancashire. Thar-Cake Monday was the first Monday following Halloween – All Saints' Day, so called because 'some of the richer sorts of persons in Lancashire use to give the poor on this day'. A quote taken from *History of the borough of Bury and neighbourhood: In the County of Lancaster*, 1874, notes, 'There was a kind of cake made in Bury and its neighbourhood during the first five days of November each year – and at no other time… This bread was designated "Thar-Cake"… "Thor Cake".'[8]

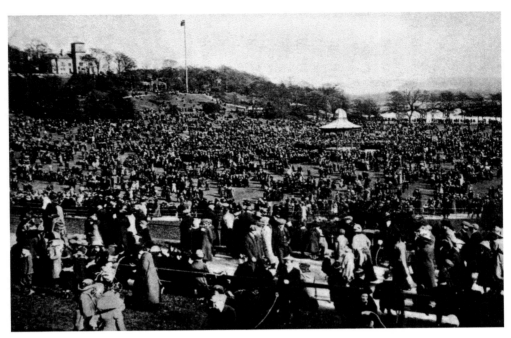

Pace-eggers at Avenham Park, Preston, 1920. (Courtesy of Preston Digital Archive)

In more modern times it became a compound of oatmeal, butter and black treacle, but originally it was made with coarsely ground or pounded grain, kneaded to a consistency with honey.

LOCAL ANCIENT FARE

One of the oldest recipes linked to Lancashire is black pudding, which was undoubtedly a dish gifted to Britain by the Romans, who mixed eggs, pine kernels, onions, leeks and blood with pepper before stuffing into a casing. This practice became very popular in the Middle Ages and somehow, somewhere along the line, got tagged with the county – possibly because Lancashire just got very good at making it!

The primrose has always been considered a good omen for a happy marriage or courtship. There was a well-known Lancashire dish that took advantage of this – a primrose pasty. This involved mixing primrose petals with sugar and a little salt, which was baked in layers of crisp rich pastry.[9] Another version I found stipulated that the pasty should consist of two discs filled with primroses and sugar, then sealed all round, making a traditional pasty shape and pricked with a couple of holes.

Oatmeal bread at one stage could be found in almost every house in Lancashire. In some towns, the so-called 'oatcake lads' would gather in groups at certain festival days throughout the year and visit their neighbourhood houses demanding an oatcake. They would rattle the door and sing

One for Peter; two for Paul;
Three for Christ, who made us all.
Up with your kettle-down with your pon;
Give us some oat cake, and we will begone.[10]

The English cookbook *Liber Cure Cocorum*, c. 1430 – a translated copy of which is stored in the archives of the British Library – is considered to have originated from the north of England, from the dialect in which it was written and is often cited as a Lancastrian text. The use of the words *ud* or *ut*, for us, *schyn* and *schun* for shall, *wyn* and *wynn* for will, as well as *tas* for takes and *tother* for that other one, are all indicative of this.[11] It was published as an appendix to a bigger text of medieval poems, titled the *boke of curtesye*. Similar recipes of this time were published in other texts such as the *Forme of Cury* and Thomas Austin's *Two Fifteenth Century Cookery Books*. But it remains a very early source of reference for food historians. The following is an ancient recipe for hagese (haggis):

Þe hert of schepe, þe nere þou take,
Þo bowel noȝt þou shalle forsake,
On þe turbilen made, and boyled wele,
Hacke alle togeder with gode persole,
Isop, saveray, þou schalle take þen,
And suet of schepe take in, I ken,
With powder of peper and egges gode wonne,
And sethe hit wele and serve hit þenne,
Loke hit be saltyd for gode menne.

```
MEYL-CRUST  APPA'  PIE                        E. Whittle
    Nah ere's a receipt as ah learned fra mi dad;
    They med it i' Mawdsla when he were a lad.
    Tek soom good cooking appas, a pahnd-happen-two
    Depending ont pie as yer plannin to do;
    Then peel em, an slice em, as thin as ya wish,
    An spread em out nice in an earthenware dish
    Wi plenty o sugar, an layers o fruit,
    Till it reyches to t top wi brown sugar to boot.
    Tek a bit o good lard, then some meyl aht o t bag
    Wi a handfull o flahr, just to ged it to clag;
    An mek a thick crust as ya lay on to t top
    An theer ya-ve a pie ye carn'd ged in a shop.
    Ya bake it in'th oven as brahn as ya please
    An Sarve it wi lashins o Lancashire cheese.
    Its olesome an good ya'll agree wi me dad
    They med it i Mawdsla when e were a lad.
                                        Margaret Greenhalgh
```

Lancashire recipe written in dialect.

In wyntur tyme when erbs ben gode,
Take powder of hom I wot in dede,
As saveray, mynt and tyme, fulle gode,
Isope and sauge I wot by þe rode.

Roughly translated:

The heart of sheep, the kidneys you take,
The bowel naught you shall forsake,
In the vortex made, and boiled well,
Hack all together with good parsley,
Hyssop, savory, you shall take then,
And suet of sheep take in, I teach,
With powder of pepper and eggs [a] good quantity
And seethe it well and serve it then,
Look it is salted for good men.
In winter time when herbs are good
Take powder of them I know indeed,
As savory, mint and thyme, quite good,
Hyssop and sage I know by the Rood.[12]

To get a sense of the sort of cooking utensils that would have been used to make the recipes published in the *Liber Cure Cocorum* we can look to Thomas Langton, who was both Sheriff of Lancashire and knighted. He was a man of considerable wealth, with an estate totalling 600 houses, 12 mills and 27,000 acres of land.[13] He owned Walton-le-Dale Manor and it is probably from one of the properties located here that an inventory of the kitchen was documented in 1573:

one dryppynge panne and one Fryinge panne
Fyve broches or spyttes great and small
two gawbeirons, two brandereths and two rackentethes of iren
two payre of pottackes [pot hooks] and two gyrde irens
Four paire of tongs and a fyer shoole [shovel]
one iren for rostynge of aples
one chaffynge dyshe (chafing dish)
One jack with rope weight and two chaines, two racks; seven spitts. One gridiron.
Grate Frame for a cinder fire, three standing chafing dishes.
Two briggs to sett kettles on, two iron frames for dripping pans.
Three iron stands to sett dishes before the fire.
Three paire of potthookes, three racken crooks.

Other than the roasting jack, which would have been very unusual in the sixteenth century, many of these items would have been typical to the kitchens of the wealthy in Lancashire during this period. 'Gawbeirons' were the frames on which the spits were supported. 'Brandereths' were timber frames. A chafing dish was just a portable food warmer, while 'gridirons' were cooking grills. A 'rackenteth' was a type of apparatus for suspending cooking utensils over the fire.[14]

Most larger houses of that time would have brewed their own beer. At Gawthorpe Hall, now owned by the National Trust but built and resided in by a long line of Shuttleworths, often employed a man from outside the estate, named Brian Lever, to come and brew for them. The brewhouses at Gawthorpe contained vast wooden tubs and vats, mash vats and combs for mixing the hot water and malt, fermenting vessels, brewing combs, stills and coolers. Arks and chests stored the meal and malt which was sifted into bolting tubs. Utensils with quirky names like eshons (wooden pails), kimblins (a tub for kneading, brewing or salting), piggins (small pails) and tundishes (a funnel for filling barrels and firkins) were used to handle the liquid after it was brewed. In the sixteenth century the estate wine was purchased from Chester and they consumed at least two cheeses a week to accompany it with.[15]

In a time before refrigeration, salting was one of the main ways in which food was preserved. At Lytham Hall in 1634, six salting tubs and five sousing (soaking) tubs were recorded. And the meat documented on-site that same year on 25 April included 'the best beeffe in the great tubb, beeffe in a lesser tubb, six barrels of Irish beeffee, six quarters more of beeffe, seven flitches and a halfe of pickled bacon, ten stone and a half of bacon'.[16]

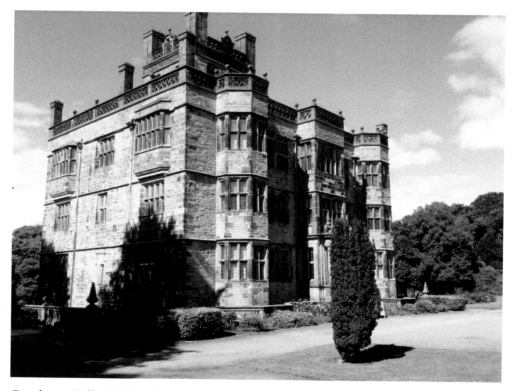

Gawthorpe Hall. (© Ellen Thompson – www.flickr.comphotoseethompson3 5527698123300)

Some of the recipes these households indulged in might have included a dish now synonymous with the county but has a much earlier provenance. The phrase 'hotpot' is not exclusive to Lancashire. It appears in numerous publications in London from the 1700s and was originally a combination of ale, brandy and sugar mixed together

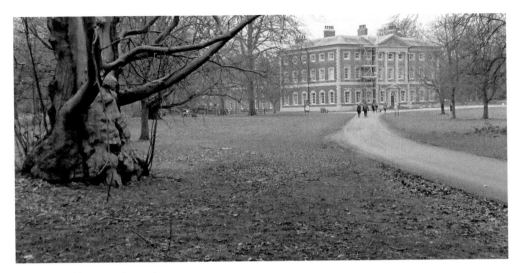

Lytham Hall. (© Nick Kay)

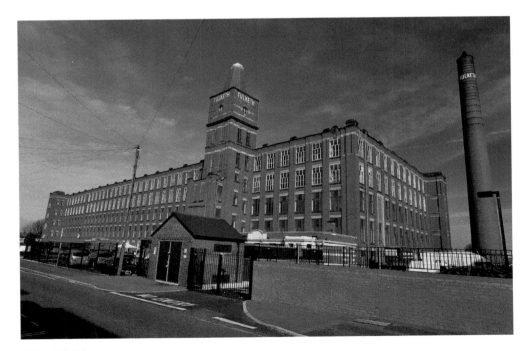

Tulketh Mill.

and heated.[17] It is not a phrase that becomes associated with the familiar Lancashire dish until the mid-1800s, with the term 'hotpot' probably emerging in the Victorian industrial era when hot pots of food were carried by a relative to the mills, to sustain their working family members.

As well as being a hot drink, 'hotchpot' in its incarnation as a meat and vegetable stew is a medieval recipe – the earliest I can find dates to around 1425 and was published in *Antiquitates Culinariae* in 1791. It uses goose meat, opposed to beef or lamb:[18]

> Goos in hochepot. Take a goos not sully rosted, and chop her on gobbettes and put hit in a. pot, and do therto brothe of fresh flesh, and take onyons and mynce hom, and do therto; take brede, and stepe hit in brothe, and drawe hit up with a lytell wyn, and do hit in the pot, and do therto pouder of pepur and of clowes, and of maces, and of raysynges of corance, and colour hit with saffron and saunders, and let thi pottage be hangynge (thick), and serve hit forthe.

A later version appears in *The Closet of Sir Kenelm Digby Knight Opened*, 1669, Kenelm Digby being a courtier, diplomat and extraordinary writer of recipes. A popular known intellectual of his time, Digby, I have discovered, also had Lancastrian descendants who died fighting in the Wars of the Roses at Towton. This is his simple recipe for hotchpot:

> To make an Hotchpot
>
> Take a piece of Brisket-beef; a piece of Mutton; a knuckle of Veal; a good Colander of pot-herbs; half minced Carrots, Onions and Cabbage a little broken. Boil all these together until they be very thick.[19]

Another medieval recipe often associated with Lancashire is braggot, braket or bragot, a recipe for which also appears in *The Closet of Sir Kenelm Digby Knight Opened*. Essentially it is honey and ale fermented together, or ale flavoured with honey and spices. This is a drink referenced as early as 1386 in Chaucer's *Miller's Tale*.

> *Hir mouth was sweete as bragot or the meeth,*
> *Or hoord of apples leyd in hey or heeth.*[20]

The drink was popular in Lancashire during Mid-Lent, later known as Mothering Sunday and also 'Braggot Sunday', as the tipple most favoured to celebrate with on this day.[21] Other counties christened this day depending on the regional preference. For example, in Hampshire it was known as Wafering Sunday, as locals indulged in sweet, creamy wafers flavoured with orange flower. It was drunk on Mid-Lent Sunday in Leigh – historically part of Lancashire, but now in Greater Manchester – and drunk in Bury, where it became most famously known as 'Bragot Sunday'. In Leigh it was tradition on this same Sunday to secretly hook a piece of coloured fabric onto a lady's gown as she walked to church.[22]

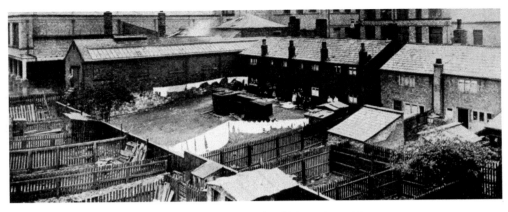

Leigh, showing the mill and tenements. *New England Magazine*, 1887.

Here is Sir Kenelm Digby's recipe. Mr or Master Webb(e), we are informed by the writer, made all the king's meads and ales. At the time, this would have been King James II.

Mr Webb's Ale and Bragot

Five Bushels of Malt will make two Hogsheads. The first running makes one very good Hogshead, but not very strong; the second is very weak. To this proportion boil a quarter of a Pound of Hops in all the water that is to make the two Hogsheads; that is, two Ounces to each Hogshead. You put your water to the Malt in the Ordinary way. Boil it well, when you come to work it with yest, take very good Beer-yest, not Ale-yest.

To make Bragot, He takes the first running of such Ale, and boils a less proportion of Honey in it, then when He makes His ordinary Meath; but dubble or triple as much spice and herbs. As for Example to twenty Gallons of the Strong-wort, he puts eight or ten pound, (according as your taste liketh more or less honey) of honey; But at least triple as much herbs, and triple as much spice as would serve such a quantity of small Mead as He made Me (For to a stronger Mead you put a greater proportion of Herbs and Spice, then to a small; by reason that you must keep it a longer time before you drink it; and the length of time mellows and tames the taste of the herbs and spice). And when it is tunned in the vessel (after working with the barm) you hang in it a bag with bruised spices (rather more then you boiled in it) which is to hang in the barrel all the while you draw it.

He makes also Mead with the second weak running of the Ale; and to this He useth the same proportions of honey, herbs and spice, as for his small Mead of pure water; and useth the same manner of boiling, working with yest, and other Circumstances, as in making of that.[23]

The mention of barm here leads into the North West indulgence for barm cakes, or those soft round, slightly flat bread rolls traditionally made from the fermented scum, or barm, that forms on the top of alcohol during distillation – an ancient form

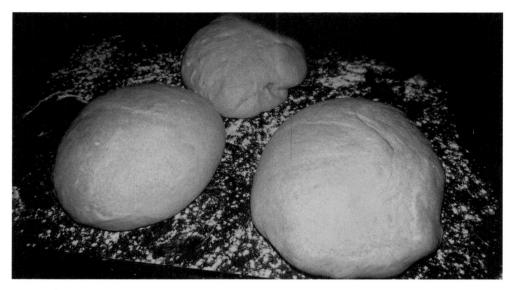

Barm cakes. (© Emma Kay)

of leavening. The good folk of Wigan even created the art of eating a pie encased in a barm, to make the pie more portable by catching the messy drippings in the bread. This 'Wigan kebab' is a more modern culinary delight, with the barm itself having much older origins.

EARLY MIGRANT INFLUENCES

Flemish weavers once settled in Bolton le Moors in the medieval period, lured by the area's vibrant local textile manufacturing. They allegedly brought with them a recipe for Hindle Wakes (Hen de la Wake or Hen of the Wake), probably as early as the twelfth century. Medieval Wake Nights were times when a body was kept in the house and in fear that Satan would seek out the corpse – lights, prayers and hymns were used to keep him away and prevent any bodies being stolen before they were committed to the ground. Wakes were also annual holiday weeks, so it's all slightly confusing. Hindle may refer to Hindley, near Wigan. No one quite knows the origin of Hindle Wakes, but I like to think that it is an ancient dish introduced by early Dutch-Belgian migrants. Things got even more complicated in 1910 when a play of the same name, tackling class divisions, about a mill girl and a mill owner's son having an affair was published by Stanley Houghton. This was later adapted for the screen and *Hindle Wakes* the movie was released in 1952. Dorothy Hartley reproduced a recipe in her 1954 book *Food in England*, claiming it to have been sourced from a family living near Wigan in 1900. Like so many food history-related books, no references are provided, so authentication remains a mystery. But I thought I would include the recipe anyway, considering all the intrigue that surrounds it.

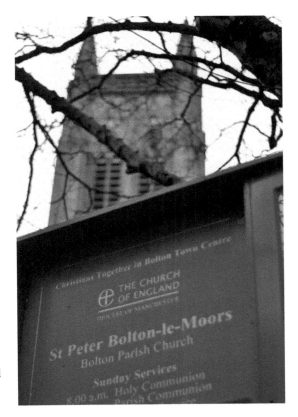

Right: Bolton-le-Moors church, Bolton.
(© Nick Kay)

Below: *Flemish Dancers*, Pieter Brueghel
the Younger, 1625. (Courtesy of
Detroit Institute of Art)

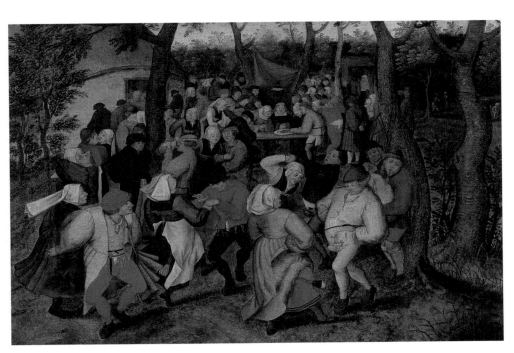

The process involved preparing an old fowl which had been hanging for some time to mature. The stuffing was made using half a loaf of dry bread mixed with twice the number of prunes. This was seasoned with salt, pepper and herbs, before adding a cupful of vinegar. Next a handful of suet is stirred into the mix and the fowl stuffed, trussed and boiled overnight in water, vinegar and brown sugar. It was then left to go completely cold before being coated with a lemon sauce and served as the main dish during the start of the wake holiday.[24]

Halton is a village in East Lancashire, thought to have Norman heritage. It was once known for its ale. Mysteries or miracle plays were popular dramatic performances during the Middle Ages. The play *Shepherds* mentions refreshment in the form of Halton ale, as being a suitable tipple to partake in during the journey east, to visit the Christ child.[25]

The stretch of coast between the Mersey and the Ribble, known as the North Meols (a Norse terms for sand dunes), was once dominated by Scandinavian communities, who crossed the Irish Sea to establish new settlements around the ninth century. They left their mark in many ways, most of which remain undocumented. Many local names derive from the old Norse language, like the 'carr' of Carr Hill and Carr Lane in Kirkham, meaning wet, marshy land. Kirkham itself originates from 'kirke', meaning church and 'ham', village.

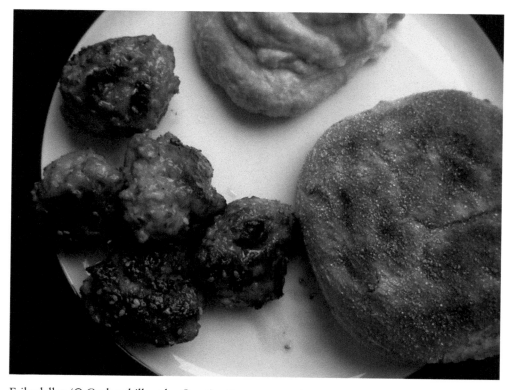

Frikadeller. (© Cyclonebill under Creative Commons 2.0)

The old name for a Viking death feast was Darval and during these feasts, Darval cakes would be served.[26] At some stage these cake/biscuits became simply Arval and they remained popular in Lancashire, as well as other northern counties. These large currant cakes were distributed to mourners during the service in an envelope sealed with black wax, superseding the old burial dole.

Clap bread or clap cake derives from the Scandinavian *klapperbrod* and *klapper-kake* (oatcakes beaten by hand) and an old local recipe from Lee Kilner, passed on to me by my mother-in-law, Lancastrian born and bred Anne Kay, is also reminiscent of the Scandinavian influences in the county, *Frikadellar/er*, being the Danish version of meatballs.

Frikadellar

½ lb mince
1 onion
1 egg
1 cup of milk
flour
salt and pepper

Method

Peel and chop onion and add to mince, egg, salt and pepper. Mix well. Add milk and stir in enough flour to make a 'Bubble Gum' consistency. Fry until golden brown – turn and fry again. Serve with raw grated carrots which have been tossed with a spoonful of sugar and a dash of lemon juice. Serve also boiled potatoes.

Um Stuarts and Georges

The seventeenth and eighteenth centuries were a period of civil unrest and massacre in Lancashire. From the battles of Preston to the Liverpool Seamen's revolt, the county was frequently split between Royalists and Parliamentarians. Locals were forced to provide food for government forces, and many had their livelihoods compromised, including the loss of mills and malt kilns destroyed in battle.

Workers, particularly colliers, rioted over low wages at a time of severe harvests and high food prices. In 1739 there was a severe frost which lasted from 23 October almost until the end of December. It hit the county hard. Ships were stranded and the rivers froze over. William Stout informs us that 'the frost killed abundance of fish, particularly eels … as also salmon'. 'It killed the cockles and sand worms'… 'Sheep starved; the ground being covered with frozen snow a month together. Many tradesmen [were] frozen out of their trades.'[1]

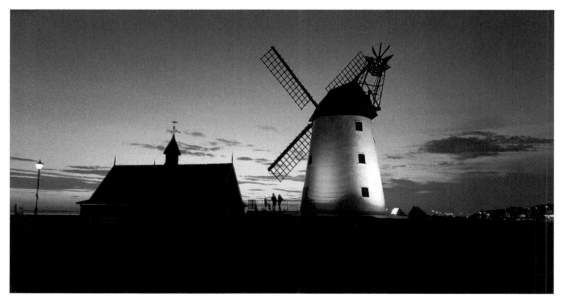

Lytham Windmill, Lytham Green. (© Nick Kay)

Famine and poverty were so extreme in parts of Lancashire in 1644, because of the ravages of the Royalist armies led by Prince Rupert, that it caught the attention of Parliament, leading to an Order being passed in the House of Commons:

…in some parts the people have hardly anything left them to cover their nakedness, or their children bread to eat; which extreme misery being represented unto the commons assembled in Parliament: It is ordered that upon the twelfth day of this Instant September, being appointed for a solemn fast, the one-half of the public collection to be made in all the churches within the cities of London, Westminster and within the lines of communication, shall be employed in the relief of those poor distressed people within the said county of Lancaster.[2]

In contrast, the ensuing century was a time of great progress, with the county often described as the first industrial region.

Despite the Romans tapping into ancient salt brines at their settlement in Northwich, Cheshire, it would be quite a few centuries later before the potential of these salt beds, in the form of rock salt, were discovered by the Smith-Barry family in the grounds of their house Marbury Hall in 1670. However, it was the Barrow family who were the principal salt merchants in Northwich, owning nine out of the seventeen brine pans, according to a treasury survey of 1733. More about the county's thriving salt industry can be found in the next chapter.[3]

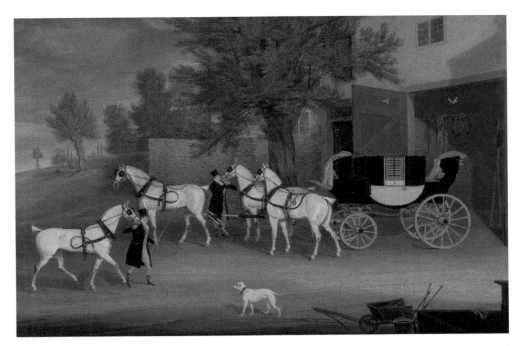

Private Drag and Grey Team at Marbury Hall, Cheshire, John Barry, 1824. (Courtesy of Yale images)

Lancashire also has a maritime heritage that equals any port city of the South. Liverpool became the location for the world's first enclosed commercial dock. As with many major port cities, luxury goods entered Liverpool and were in demand across all classes of society way before the Industrial Revolution. These included tea from China, spices, coffee, West Indian sugar and Mexican chocolate.

Liverpool became a significant maritime town in the 1700s, with numerous transient communities leaving their impression on the landscape, but its slave trading history has also left the city with a bitter legacy.

Irish migrants started descending on Liverpool as early as the 1798 rising. This continued with the subsequent Irish famines of the nineteenth century and the depression of the 1920s and '30s.

Wet Nellie/Wet Neller, also known in its drier form elsewhere in the country as Nelson Cake or Chester Cake, is a favourite of Liverpool. It is a sort of exaggerated bread and butter pudding with currants. There are a few stories that circulate about Wet Nellie, but this is one of my favourites. Legend has it that the Liverpool Cocoa Rooms that sprang up all around the city in the nineteenth century, managed by the temperance movement, decided to make a standard bread and butter pudding recipe go a bit further and added water or diluted condensed milk. This only served to make it a soggy mess, but when cooked it became solid enough to cut. With the Chester Cake version, a thin layer of pastry was added to both the top and bottom.[4] Undoubtedly the Chester Cake derives from Ireland, which is probably how it made its way into Liverpool, opposed to the county seat of Cheshire.

Chester Cake

750 g [about one standard size loaf] Stale, good-quality sliced white bread soaked overnight in water to cover

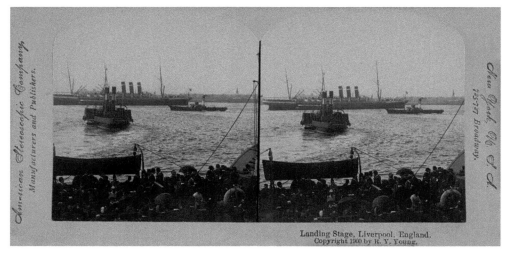

Landing Stage Liverpool, 1900. (Courtesy of the Library of Congress)

2 tbsp sugar
1 tbsp black treacle or molasses
2 tsp apple pie spice
115 g sultanas
short crust pastry
white flour for dusting
1 egg yolk, lightly beaten with 1 tsp cold water

Preheat the oven to 450 degrees F/230 degrees Celsius (Gas Mark 8)

Squeeze the water from the bread until it's dryish, then put the bread into a medium bowl. Add the sugar, treacle or molasses, apple pie spice and sultanas and mix together well. Divide pastry dough into 2 uneven pieces: three-quarters for the bottom crust and one-quarter for the top crust. Roll out the larger piece of dough on a lightly floured board to a thickness of about ¼ in/6.5mm to fit into bottom and up the sides of a loaf pan. Lightly press the dough into the pan, prick all over with a fork and spoon in the bread filling.

Roll out the remaining piece of dough on a lightly floured board into a 5x10 in/12x 25 cm rectangle about ¼ in/6.5 mm thick and carefully lay it on top of the filling. Crimp the edges and brush the pastry top with the egg wash. Prick the top crust all over with a fork. Bake for 20 minutes; then reduce the oven temperature 400 F/200 c (Gas Mark 6) and bake for 20 minutes more. Allow to cool in the pan before serving.

To serve, turn the cake out of the pan and cut into slices 1 ½ to 2 in/4 to 5 cm thick.[5]

There are many old dishes particular to Liverpool. Pea whack/wack is a name this area gave to pea and ham soup – whack meaning a portion or share of. One of the best recipes I have found for pea and ham soup from a local writer is that provided by Elizabeth Raffald. Elizabeth Raffald (née Whittaker) was an extraordinary person who deserves greater recognition. Born in Doncaster in 1733, she went into service as housekeeper to Lady Elizabeth Warburton at Arley Hall and Gardens in Cheshire. After marrying Arley's head gardener, John Raffald, she moved to Manchester where, over the next eighteen years, she reportedly ran two pubs, two coffee shops, an indoor and outdoor catering business, delivered cookery lessons and opened Manchester's first registry office – an employment agency for servants. She also embarked on a career in journalism, taking on one newspaper and founding another, *Prescott's Journal*, not to mention compiling a detailed directory of Manchester and Salford in 1772.[6] Elizabeth wrote one of the most successful books of her time (in terms of sales), for which she is now chiefly remembered. The following recipe is taken from this book, *The Experienced English Housekeeper*:

To make Green-Pea Soup

Shell a peck of peas and boil them in spring water till they are soft; then work them through a hair sieve; take the water that your peas were boiled in, and put in a knuckle of veal three slices of ham, and cut two carrots, a turnip, and a few beet

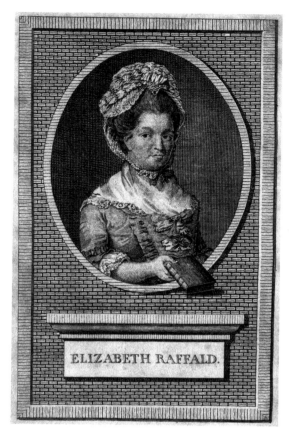

Left: Elizabeth Raffald.

Below: Cattle market, Salford. (Courtesy of Mark Crombie)

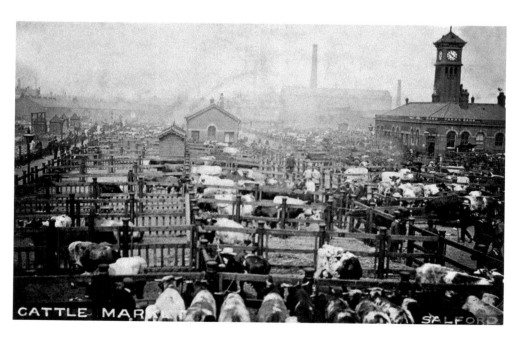

leaves shred small; add a little more water to the meat; set it over the fire, and let it boil one hour and a half; then strain the gravy into a bowl, and mix it with the pulp, and put in a little juice of spinage, which must be beat and squeezed through a cloth; put in as much as will make it look a pretty color; then give it a gentle boil, which will take off the taste of the spinage; slice in the whitest part of a head of celery; put in a lump of sugar the size of a walnut; take a slice of bread, and cut it in little square pieces; cut a little bacon in the same way; fry them a light brown in fresh butter; cut a large cabbage lettuce in slices; fry it after the other; put it in the tureen with the fried bread and bacon; have ready boiled as for eating, a pint of young peas, and put them in the soup, with a little chopped mint if you like it, and pour it into your tureen.[7]

In fact, peas were very important to Lancashire, not just in soups and on the side as a mushy accompaniment, heralding back to the days of the ancient dish of pease pudding. Carlin peas are small and brown also known as maple peas, pigeon peas, brown peas, and black/grey badgers. The eating of them at Lent was less to do with the religious ceremony and more about the Civil War of 1644, when people were starving from lack of food. These little dark-coloured peas were fried in butter or meat fat and were well seasoned, providing good, accessible fodder.

Before the level of progress began to alter the industrial landscape of Lancashire, many locals working in the food and drink trade made their way south to London in search of better employment opportunities, away from the conflicts and poverty. Sadly, as the records demonstrate, these people frequently found themselves turning to crime to survive.

Richard Whitworth was from Lancashire and the son of a butcher who continued in this trade before ending up in London. In 1693 he stole sixty-nine gold coins and 180 pounds in money after breaking into a house in Stepney. He was executed at Tyburn for his crimes.[8] Elizabeth Tethrington, also from Lancashire, left to work in the London markets selling fruit and herbs. It appears she carried out a spot of highway robbery on the side, leading to her execution at just nineteen years of age at Tyburn in 1695. It was a strange crime that she was tried for – stripping a child of six years of all her clothes, presumably to sell.[9] And Laurence Wilkinson was the son of a farmer in Lancashire who left the homestead, marrying against the wishes of his family and running a victualing house near Smithfield Market, London, where he traded in counterfeit money. For his crimes he was also executed at Tyburn in 1697.[10]

It wasn't just the runaways to London that got up to mischief in the county. One of the biggest and grisliest of Lancashire's exports is its witches, the stories of which continue to define the area of Pendle today.

Of two of the lesser heights positioned in the shadow of Pendle Hill, Stang Top Moor and Wheathead Height, the latter, according to John A. Clayton, includes the areas known as Lower and Higher Wheathead. An estate plan of Lower Wheathead revealed a piece of land once known as Oastgate Clough – oast meaning 'hop drying kiln' and suggesting evidence of grain-related practices which would have involved the treatment and brewing of both wheat and oats. In nearby Admergill, additional evidence of corn-drying operations on a significant scale have been unearthed,

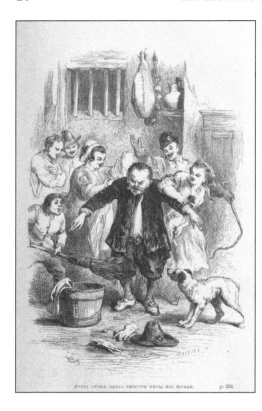

Left: *The Lancashire Witches*, 1854. (Courtesy of the British Library)

Below: Rossendale Valley towards Pendle Hill.

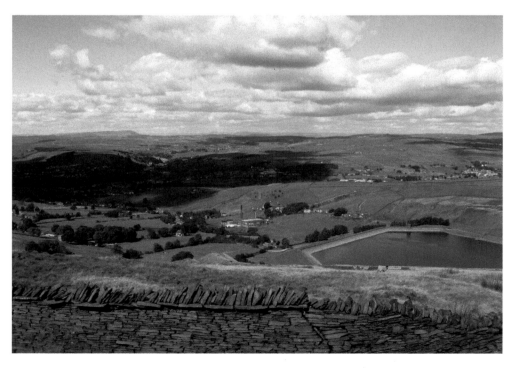

including grooved rack stones. One of the fields in the Admergill estate was also known as Mill Field, suggesting the one-time presence of a corn mill, perhaps used on a commercial scale.[11] Pendle probate inventories from the seventeenth century, identified by Robert Poole, record agricultural land that included oats, wheat and barley.[12] In fact, one of the central villages involved in the Pendle witch trials was Wheatley Lane, its very name suggestive of what may have grown in abundance there, although this has been disputed by some as being land not worthy of wheat cultivation, attributing the original name to Wethead. A confession from an accused witch, Margaret Johnson, living in Marsden in the parish of Whalley, around 8 miles from Wheatley Lane, offered the following account:

> That betwixt seaven or eight yeares since she beinge in her owne house in Marsden in a greate passion of anger and discontent, and withal pressed with some want, there appeared unto her a spirit or devil in the similitude and propor- tion of a man, aparelled in a suite of black, tied about with silk points, who offered that yf shee would give him her soule, hee would supplie all her wants, and bringe to her whatsoever shee did neede, and at her appointment would in revenge either kill or hurt whom or what shee desired, were it man or beast.[13]

What is particularly striking about the Pendle witches is that they resemble other famous historical trials; stories of wild hallucinations, convulsions and various forms of mania, together with the physical manifestation of 'marks of the devil'. It is trials such as the ones that took place in Salem, Massachusetts, in the 1600s; in Chelmsford, Essex in the 1500s; the Pappenheimers of Bavaria in 1600; and so on that potentially all identify with the presence of Ergot poisoning.

Ergotism can produce physical deformities caused by gangrene, in addition to a variety of symptoms including severe itching, spasms, nausea and psychosis. It is a type of poisoning caused by infected grains that can have long-term effects. It also remained undiagnosed in the seventeenth and eighteenth centuries. The signs and symptoms consistent with ergotism could very easily have been mistaken for witchcraft and demonism in superstitious times. It is even transferrable from mother to child. This theory was first proffered by the psychologist Linnda Caporael with reference to her research into the Salem witch trials.

In order to thrive, the fungus *claviceps purpurea* needs damp weather conditions and cool temperatures, in fields where cereal crops are not frequently rotated or deeply ploughed. Late medieval more northerly locations with colder climates would have been perfect breeding grounds. It is possible that the agricultural landscapes of Pendle and its surrounds could quite easily account for some of the unusual incidents that took place there in the 1600s.

It's worth mentioning that Pendle had its own local term for a kneading board called a 'Bagbread', which was specifically used to prepare oatcakes. Another type of board was a spittle, with a handle used to turn the dough of the oatcake onto the bakestone. Oatmeal and barley were the main cereals grown in this district and wheat was only eaten during special occasions or by yeoman families. Bread 'flekes' or bread 'cratches' were frames or racks used to dry oatcakes on.[14] There are numerous regional specific dishes like bunnocks, once a common term in North Lancashire for a small cake, the principal ingredients of which were oatmeal and treacle. The cakes varied in size from 2 to 4 inches in diameter. Brewis is often associated with Oldham and Bolton in Lancashire. It was an oatcake or bread toasted and soaked in broth or stew. The Welsh have their own version, but considering the geographic proximity to Wales this is unsurprising.

Hakin is a Cumberland dish, but also prepared by many across Lancashire once upon a time. It was popular on Christmas Day morning for breakfast.

> Take the Bag or Paunch of a Calf, and wash it, and clean it well with Water and Salt; then take some Beef-Suet, and shred it small, and shred some Apples, after they are pared and cored, very small. Then put in some Sugar, and some Spice beaten small, a little Lemon-Peel cut very fine, and a little Salt, and a good quantity of Grots, or whole Oat-meal, steep'd a Night in Milk; then mix these all together, and add as many Currans pick'd clean from the Stalks, and rubb'd in a coarse Cloth; but let them not be wash'd. And when you have all ready, mix them together, and put them into the Calf's-Bag, and tye them up, and boil them till they are enough. You may, if you will, mix up with the whole, some Eggs beaten, which will help to bind it. This is our Custom to have ready, at the opening of the Doors, on *Christmas*-Day in the Morning. It is esteem'd here; but all that I can say to you of it, is, that it eats somewhat like a *Christmas*-Pye, or is somewhat like that boil'd. I had forgot to say, that with the rest of the Ingredients, there should be some Lean of tender Beef minced small.[15]

Aughton Pudding Festival is held every twenty-one years in the village of Aughton near Ormskirk. It dates to at least 1782 – maybe earlier – traditionally to see who could bake the biggest pudding. William Sanderson, a poet of the Regency period from Lancaster, wrote a piece of verse all about the pudding:

> There were raisins, currants and figs,
> Sugar, almonds, plums, lemons and spice,
> All the choice of what came in three brigs,
> For its cargo each brig going twice.
> When all these were properly mixed,
> There was poured in a hogshead of rum,
> On the cask head this label was fix'd,
> From Jamaica on purpose 'tis come.
>
> Sing hey for Aughton's brave pudding
> For Aughton's brave pudding sing ho,
> In the spring time when roses are budding,
> To Aughton we'll all of us go
>
> For ten days five fat bakers toil'd,
> A kneading the flour into dough,

Which was in a ward boiler boil'd,
Just a fortnight to make it enough.
This pudding was twenty feet long,
Six thick and just eighteen feet round,
And a dozen young men stout and strong,
Could scarcely raise it from the ground.

The poem continues for a further three verses. The chorus in between and at the end ends with 'The next time the pudding is made, I hope I may be there to taste.'[16] The last festival was in 2013. I sincerely hope the spirit of tradition maintains into 2034 and I too will be around to taste its delights.

Although Blackpool did not really emerge until the 1600s as a place of any real substance, many of its surrounding districts are mentioned in the Domesday Book. Before *blackpoole*, so named for its strip of peaty-coloured water, became the sea-bathing, all-curing destination for the wealthier classes of the 1700s, or the glamorous and entertaining seaside holiday resort of the nineteenth century, it was simply a mass of sand hills and common land, eventually with a system of road networks linking it to Lytham and St Annes. In the latter half of the 1700s Blackpool began to be known for its live music concerts, the start of its legacy as a performance town. It's heritage is thankfully now being preserved and interpreted by the new 'Showtown' museum. *The Rise and Growth of Blackpool* informs us that in the 1780s,

To reach Blackpool, you also could take the Carlisle Roval Mail Coach, through Preston, or the Lancaster coach which left every Monday, Wed-nesday and Friday, at 6 o'clock, passing through Bolton, Chorley, and Preston; the former con-ducted by Dixon and Co., and starting from the Swan Inn, Market Street Lane.[17]

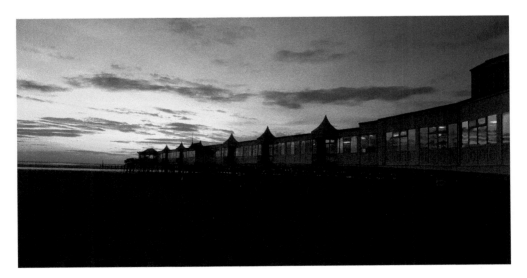

Lytham St Annes Pier. (© Nick Kay)

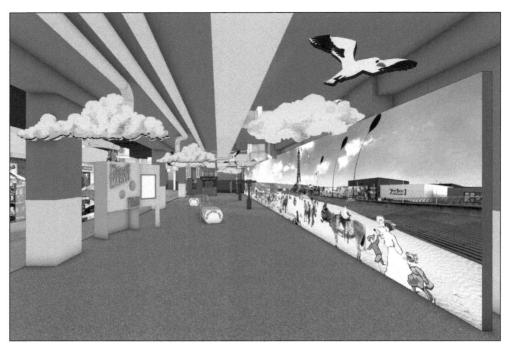

Showtown *Seaside* Gallery. (© Casson Mann. Courtesy of Blackpool Council)

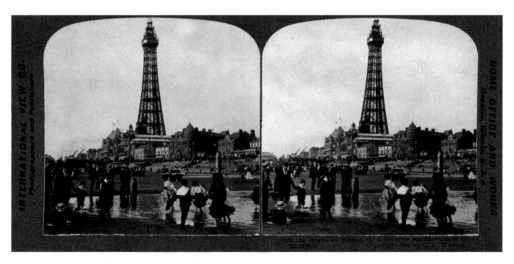

Blackpool, 1905. (Courtesy of the Library of Congress)

The oldest habitation in Blackpool was Fox Hall, once reconditioned into a public house and now sadly demolished, despite its historical importance. The family who built it in the 1600s were the Tyldesleys and Thomas Tyldesley, the grandson of the Royalist general Sir Thomas Tyldesley, kept a journal from 1712 to 1714 which provides tremendous insight into life in early, pre-established Blackpool. There was a great deal of fishing and hunting recorded. Carp and tench catches are abundant, along with hares, wading birds, wildfowl, ducks and even otters. Thomas talks of visiting a coffee house in Preston in 1712, where a cup cost him two old pence – around eighty-seven pence today. His noted food purchases over the years included cockles, eggs, fish, ducks, veal, beef, cheese (from Wigan), mutton, salmon, calves' heads, syllabubs, cauliflowers, cabbages, strawberries, carrots, black cherries, raspberries and potatoes, which along with William Stout from Lancaster's account in 1725, noting that potatoes were 'plenty and cheap, from 9s. 6d. to 3s. a load', is good evidence to suggest that they were being richly cultivated in the region at this time.[18]

The killing of pigs was considered a great sport back in the eighteenth century and Thomas notes that he and his family spent two old pence each on tickets for a 'pige feast' in 1714. He also mentions dining on 'buttred eges'. A very popular dish of the time, essentially this was scrambled eggs beaten on the fire with butter and served on toast. Scrambled eggs were gifted to British cuisine by the Romans, who frequently ate them mixed in with fish. One of the earliest references to 'buttered eggs' appears in the English professional cook Robert May's *The Accomplisht Cook*, published in 1660. He recommends several versions; from the simple method we are all familiar with today, to more elaborate methods adding sugar, lamb gravy, rose water and spices. There is even an option for buttered eggs with grated lemon peel, topped with cheese.

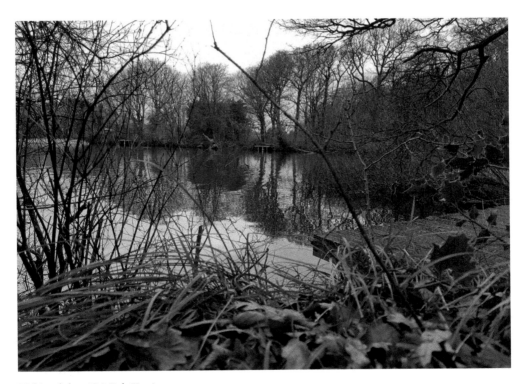

Fishing lake. (© Nick Kay)

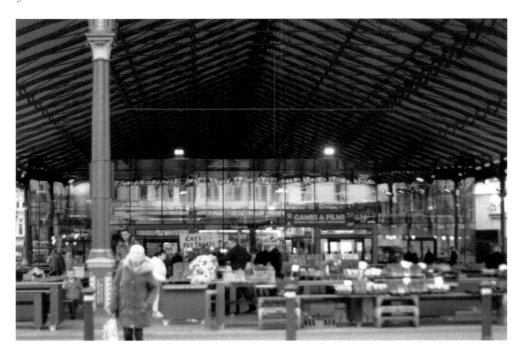

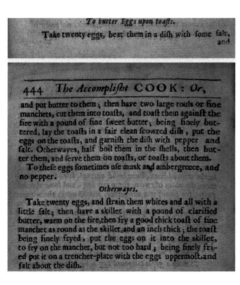

Above: Preston outdoor market. (© Nick Kay)

Left: Recipe for buttered eggs from
The Accomplisht Cook, Robert May.

Thomas Tyldesley went on to marry Eleanor, the daughter of Thomas Holcroft of Holcroft Hall, Culcheth. They had ten children. He is buried at Garstang.

Despite Blackpool's current separate administration, it remains part of the Fylde Coast, a substantial geographical region encompassing coastal towns like Fleetwood, Thornton and Cleveleys, together with numerous rural villages including Warton, Freckleton and Wrea Green among others. This area was known for its browis, throdkins, cockles, jannocks and pikelins (a muffin) in the 1700s, with parsnips and peas being the main vegetables, along with beans and rye bread.[19]

Browis is a sort of barley soup with a medieval heritage, not particularly specific to Lancashire; whereas throdkins certainly seem to have originated in the county and in the Fylde district. It may derive from the Norse word *throdden*, meaning to grow or thrive and is suggestive of those Scandinavian influences mentioned in chapter one. It was a staple dish of oatmeal and water kneaded together and pushed into a deep plate, around an inch and a half thick. The surface was covered in slices of bacon fat before being baked.[20] I have also heard that this was sometimes served with treacle. A jannock is a thick, unleavened oatcake which has been attributed to the Flemish refugees in Lancashire of old. It is similar to the havercake. 'Havercake Lads' being a Lancashire regiment who fought in the Boer War. Originating in East Lancashire, the havercake

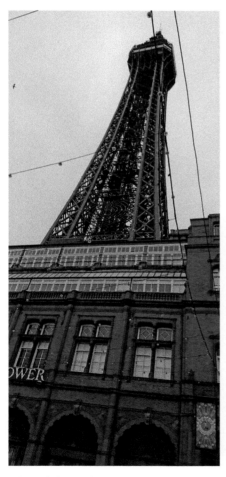 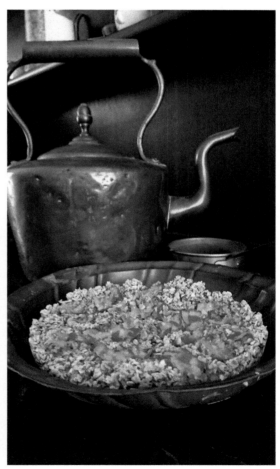

Above left: Blackpool Tower. (© Emma Kay)

Above right: Throdkin. (© Emma Kay)

was an oatcake baked on a stone slab called a 'back stone'. This was left to dry out and taken as sustenance for the road by young soldiers. Oatmeal porridge and oatcake played a significant part in the diet of people from Lancashire and great pride was taken over the name of havercake.[21]

Cockles were, together with other shellfish like shrimps, a significant source of income for Lancashire. James Baxter and Son of Morecambe Bay was founded in 1799. Still a family firm, it retains the title of the oldest company of its kind in the country. Fleetwood was at one time the third largest fishing port in Britain. Now, all that remains of this legacy is the town's dedicated and financially challenged museum, housed in the former Customs House. Once a thriving hive of industry, Fleetwood relies on its main employer, Fisherman's Friend, and the reputation of its namesake football team. Just as I love Blackpool, I also find the faded glory and pride of Fleetwood both utterly fascinating and sad in equal measures. They are towns that once contributed so much and are now in desperate need of regeneration. If you are reading this book and you have never visited the Lancashire coast, please do consider it. There is so much history, so many stories in danger of being forgotten.

The Country Housewife and Lady's Director in the Management of a House, and the Delights and Profits of a Farm by Richard Bradley written in 1732 includes a collection of recipes from a variety of farmers across the country, recorded by the author. They include one from Mrs R. S. of Preston – 'To Pott Trouts':

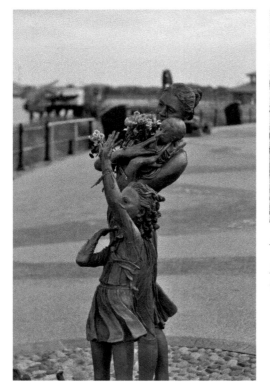

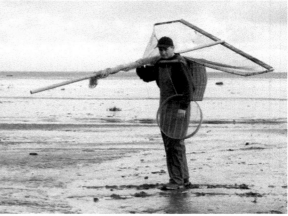

Above: Lancashire shrimper.

Left: Fleetwood memorial to those lost at sea. (© Nick Kay)

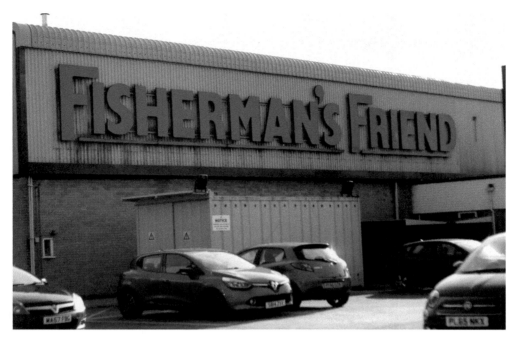

Fisherman's Friend, Fleetwood. (© Nick Kay)

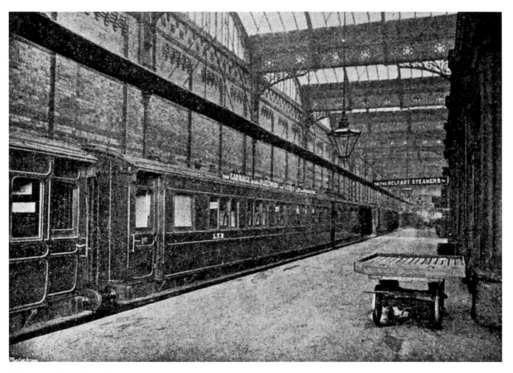

Fleetwood rail station.

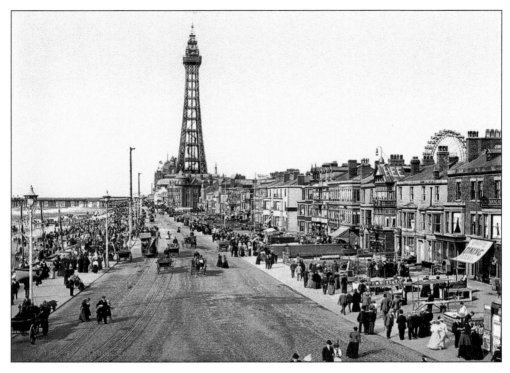

Promenade Blackpool *c.* 1890. (Courtesy of the Library of Congress)

To pott Trouts. From Mrs. *R. S.* of *Preston* in *Lancashire.*

Scale and clean your Trouts very well, wash them in Vinegar, and slit them down the Back, after which put Pepper and Salt into the Incision, and on their Outsides, and let them lie upon a Dish three Hours; then lay them in an earthen glaz'd Pan, with pieces of Butter upon them, and put them in an Oven two Hours, if they are Trouts fourteen Inches long, or less in proportion, taking care to tie some Paper close over the Pan. When this is done, take away from them all the Liquor, and put them in a Pot, and as soon as they are quite cold, pour some clarified Butter upon them to cover them: These will eat as well as potted Charrs. Some will take out the Bone upon slitting the Back, and these have been often taken for Charrs; tho' I don't know above two Places where the Charrs are, one is a Pool where a River or Brook runs thro' in *Lancashire*, and the other is in a Pool at *Naant*, within four Miles of *Caernarvon*. But the Charr is of the Trout kind, and it must be a good judge in Fish to distinguish one from another; however, there is some small difference, which the Criticks in fishing take notice of.

Fish may also be kept in Pickle several Weeks, as the Jack and Trout especially are agreeable Varieties.[22]

There is one other culinary narrative of local legend to add to this chapter – the royal menu for the Sunday dinner and supper prepared for King James I at Houghton Tower, Preston, by Bishop Morton, the Bishop of Chester, on 17 August 1617. Records of what was prepared have survived, a copy of which appeared in the journals of 1617 to

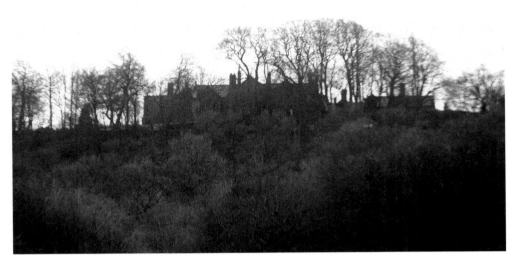

Houghton Tower. (© Nick Kay)

1619 by Nicholas Assheton, a county squire from Clitheroe. An early printed version from 1790 recently sold at auction for £3,000.

> FIRST COURSE: Pullets boiled capon mutton, boiled chickens shoulder of mutton, roast clucks, boiled loin of veal, roast pullets, haunch of venison, roast burred capon pasty of venison, hot roast turkey veal, burred swan roast, one; and one for to-morrow chicken pye, hot goose, roasted rabbits, cold jiggits of mutton, boiled snipe pye breast of veal, boiled capons, roast pullet beef, roast tongue pye, cold sprod, boiled herons roast, cold curlew pye, cold mince pye, hot custards, pig. roast.
>
> SECOND COURSE: Hot pheasant, one; and one for the king quails, six for the king partridge poults artichoke pye chickens curlews, roast peas, buttered rabbits duck plovers red deer pye pig, burred hot herons, roast, three of a dish lamb, roast gammon of bacon pigeons, roast made dish chicken, burred pear tart pullets and grease dried tongues turkey pye pheasant pye pheasant tart hogs' cheeks, dried turkey chicks, cold.

The dinner was followed, about four o'clock, by piping and rushbearing with a later supper consisting of various roast and boiled chickens, turkeys, venison pasties, quails, pigeons, tongue, rabbits and so on. A masque was laid on for the king in the gardens, including dances and speeches.[23]

There is a misleading belief that one speech during the king's visit to Houghton led to the infamous knighting of a piece of beef, with James I allegedly announcing, 'Sir Loin', thereby christening the phrase sirloin, to a cut of steak. However, there is another story of Henry VIII also knighting a loin of beef several hundred years earlier over a bet to see whether the Abbot of Reading could become hungry enough to eat as much beef as the king. In fact, neither is probably true. The word *surloign*, meaning 'above the loin', is of French origin and can be traced back to at least 1554.[24]

3

Brass, Booths and Boats

The Victorian and Edwardian eras were, like for many other counties, boom times. But for the labouring classes times were tough, with poor working conditions and workplace rights still only on the cusp of recognition. Blake's 'dark, Satanic Mills' were not far from the truth as they dominated the landscapes of Britain, representing capitalist ideologies and the repressing of culture.

Children played a significant role in getting the midday meal out to their working parents and siblings. William Woodruff recalls of the cotton mills:

> The meal, a stew of meat, potatoes and vegetables, was cooked by mother the night before. Each person took their filled basin to work and left it on a large stove in the warehouse. Before noon the basins were hotted up, hence hot pot. I would leave school at 11.45 am, run along the river to the mill and locate my family's dinners...

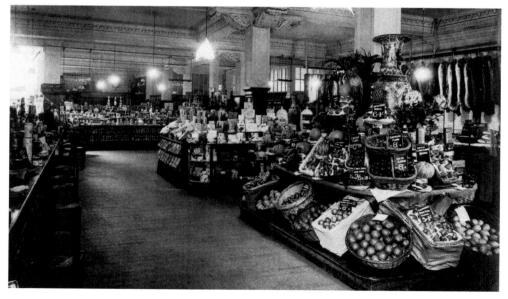

Booths café and shop, Fishergate, Preston, 1933. (Courtesy of Preston Digital Archive)

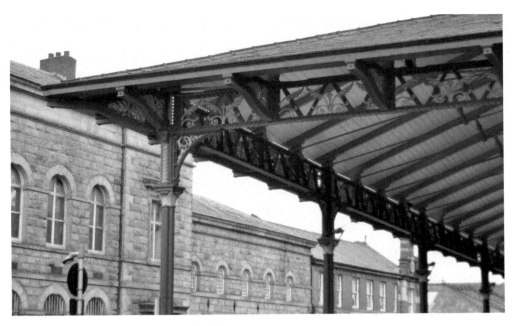

Victorian market awning, Preston. (© Nick Kay)

I placed each basin in my cap because it was scalding hot, and ran with it through the mill to each family member's workplace ... always running in and out of the mills. I had plenty of opportunity to learn about textile machinery.[1]

Cotton operatives typically worked from 6 a.m. to 6 p.m., with an hour for lunch. In 1842 the highest weekly wage for a child under thirteen working was 11 shillings, the lowest, 1s.6d employed in Lancashire collieries. In parts of Lancashire it was not unusual to employ children as young as four or five.[2] The Cotton Famine of the 1860s generated mass unemployment, resulting in impoverished communities, many of which found themselves reliant on handouts from local relief committees. Streams of people queued outside soup kitchens and many families survived on just two bowls of Indian meal porridge a day.[3] Indian meal was maize, which was cheaper to cultivate than wheat or oats.

Fall River cotton mills, Massachusetts in Newport, America, offered many millworkers living and working in harsh conditions in Burnley and Blackburn the opportunity to start a new life working in the burgeoning textile industry across the Atlantic. Advertisements promising a glamorous location, better housing and cleaner living were incentive enough for many Lancastrians to make the move. The reality however was very different. On arrival, working migrants would have been confronted with cramped living spaces, low wages and dehumanizing workplaces. The landscape may have been located at the mouth of a river, but the size of the mills and the thousands of wood-framed tenements blocked out any of the aesthetics. One hopeless environment would simply have been replaced with another.

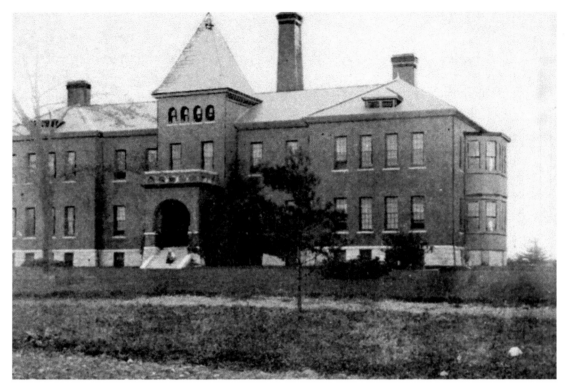

Fall River, Massachusetts.

Fall River was often referred to as 'hills, mills and pork pies and dinner pails'[4] after the English introduced their pork pies and fondness for a hearty meal.

Hartley's store initially opened in Main Street, Fall River, specialising in pork pies, introduced by British migrants. Deep-dish savoury pies were their speciality when the shop opened in 1900. It was started by Thomas Hartley, who was almost certainly from Lancashire. He worked in a textile mill, then opened a fish and chip shop, before finding success with his pies.

Thomas's son opened another similar shop in Lincoln, Rhode Island, in 1954 and there is another store in Somerset, Massachusetts, established in 1902. The recipe was sold by his grandson Harold to the store owners in Somerset. All the stores continue to trade today. In 1921 Thomas Hartley's estate is listed in the city documents with a value of £100,000.[5] I can find little about the shop itself in the 1900s and certainly Hartley was not the only local pork pie maker, as there was at least one other, William Goddard, trading in the town at this time.[6]

Incidentally, it is understood that a man from Clitheroe, Walter Beattie, introduced Fall River to the game of soccer back in the nineteenth century. They used a 'tar barrel' or an inflated black rubber ball, locked with a key, to play with. He went on, together with his brother, to train a succession of young men in the game, creating teams and medal winners.[7]

SEA AND SALT

Lancashire is a maritime county which often gets forgotten, and Liverpool, once part of this enormous eclectic landscape, was arguably one of the greatest commercial seaports in the world. In the vein of the successful Cornish blockbuster *Fisherman's Friends*, it's no wonder that numerous other old shanty singers, including the likes of the Sunderland Point sea shanty crew and the Lytham St Annes shanty crew continue today to entertain the public with musical chants dedicated to those who served at sea in numerous capacities, fishing being one of the main occupations for local men in the past. In the 1960s, local playwright and songwriter Ron Baxter, together with several colleagues, wrote lyrics dedicated to the fishing industry in Fleetwood, including a song inspired by an old trawler heading for the breaker's yard, called *Lord Middleton*, the final verse of which goes:

No more will she pass the Morecambe Light - no more will her siren sound;
No more will her engine pound the night - no more will she be outward bound;
No more will she wander the icy seas, nor her smokestack smear the sky;
For over there in the old scrap-yard, the *Lord Middleton* must die.[8]

Victorian fishing boats like the *Lancashire Nobby* were used along the north-west coast of England as shrimp trawlers up until the Second World War. Typically, they ranged from anywhere between 25 feet and 45 feet. There was a specific Morecambe Bay *Nobby* that operated between the ports of Barrow, Morecambe, Fleetwood and Heysham, as well as the Lancashire coast, Liverpool, Southport and St Annes.[9]

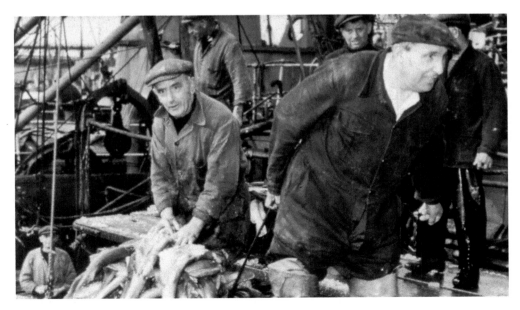

Fleetwood fishermen. (Courtesy of Fleetwood Museum)

Red Charger: A Trip on the Arctic Fishing Grounds, written in 1950 by George Goldsmith Carter, tells the story of a Fleetwood trawler of the same name, skippered by Bobby Nash, fishing the Arctic waters. The conditions were harsh and the work arduous. The barren, cold seascape gives way to stories of fishermen seeing phantom, spectral trawlers in remote, isolated locations and food supplies on board running short. *Red Charger* caught haddock and cod and a strange fish called tusk, a member of the cod family. Live coral and a great deal of 'duff' was hauled up, but crabs and lobsters were hard to come by. Carter regales skipper Nash singing a shanty on board the *Red Charger's* voyage, with verses including:

Now this Fleetwood skipper's a terrible man,
Gets a huge bag of ducks then drops down a dann;
And then he will tow till his deckies are through...

Cos your world is confined to a very small space
And the fo'c'sle's your only amusement place.

When a miner goes home and his day's work is done
He can dress himself up and go out for some fun!
The same with a weaver with his eight-hour day,
Still he grumbles and growls in his own tin-pot way...

When into your bunk, wet and weary you roll,
Then the skipper sings out, "Now we're going to haul!"
You folks, snug on shore, don't know how hard life can be
For the good-natured deckies 'way out on the sea —[10]

The Lancashire coastline did not only provide fish and seafood. It was also gifted an abundance of salt. There are numerous pockets of brine extraction dotted around, most notably at Stalmine, which was active from 1872 to 1994.

The Fleetwood Salt Company established itself in 1883, tapping into the salt fields of Preesall. In 1890 the company was taken over by the United Alkali Company and the race was on to build the county's salt mining empire. Built to the north of the salt marshes on the eastern bank of the River Wyre, bore holes were drilled, reservoirs with pipelines constructed, workers' cottages sprang up and tunnels built. A pipeline under the River Wyre enabled salt to be exported directly from Fleetwood, via ships setting off at a rate of over one a week. The mine was annually producing some 140,000 tons of rock salt by 1905, transported directly by the Preston and Wyre Railway Company to the newly built jetty on the Wyre. But the increasing strain on the land due to subsistence from the mining over many years took its toll.[11] Several accidents with casualties occurred in the Preesall mines from explosions, flying lumps of rock salt, timber and falling salt to men being trapped by the bogies that were used to carry the salt. The United Alkali Company became merged into ICI, who required access to large salt reserves. Ironically, almost as soon as the merger took place in 1930, the mines had to close, due to structural dissolving and three years later a significant area subsided into the brine reservoir.[12] The mines once yielded a thousand tons of salt for the table and commercial purposes, every week, employing some 300 people.[13] Rosemary Hogarth has an extensive knowledge of the history of Preesall salt which has informed a great many publications over the years, enabling the stories to live on. She is also the great-niece of the last surviving salt miner in the town, Harold Daniels.

SAY 'CHEESE'!

Jay Rayner once said, 'I seriously bloody hate Lancashire cheese. I would rather stay in and chew my own toenails than have to eat the stuff.'[14] Cheesemaking in Lancashire can be traced back as far as the twelfth century when in 1199 King John granted Preston a royal charter to host an annual cheese fair. There are three types of Lancashire cheese: creamy, tasty and crumbly.

The formal traditional method for making Lancashire cheese was established by Joseph Gornall of Cabus in Garstang and later, Pilling. Joseph first spoke about the insufficiencies with dairy produce on farms throughout the county in 1892 at a meeting of the Lancashire Tenant Farmers' Association. He spent a great deal of time visiting farms and was shocked by their lack of proper equipment, poor storage and other conveniences which were making for badly produced cheese and butter. Milk was often being kept overnight in damp, unsuitable rooms alongside other foodstuffs which were liable to taint it. This spoiled both the cheese and butter.

Many farms in Lancashire didn't have access to proper clean water, which also affected the dairy products. At this time, cheesemaking courses were taking off around the county, but many farmers lacked the proper appliances with which to follow their

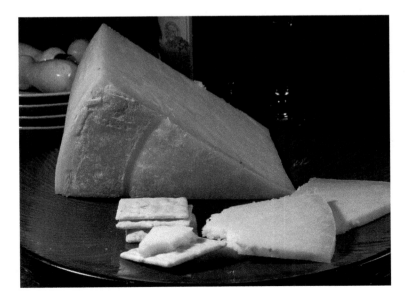

Lancashire cheese.

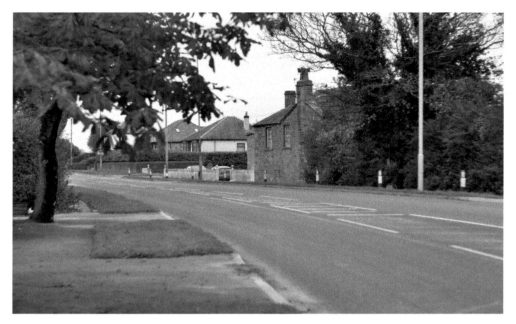

Road to Pilling. (© Nick Kay)

training with.[15] By 1892 Joseph had patented his Cheesemaker, which was 'specially adapted for the making of Lancashire cheese'. It was described as 'The cheese-maker's friend', requiring 'not half the labour. Little washing-up. Does its work quickly. Also, more curd of better quality. Easy to learn. Compact and portable. Very durable. Also reasonable in price.' It was exhibited at the Preston Cheese Fair on 28 February 1893.[16] This invention quickly became universal.

Here is a recipe for cheese pudding taken from the parish of St Michael's Church, Weeton. It originally came from the village policeman's house.

Cheese Pudding

6-8 slices of bread and butter
2 eggs
Salt and pepper
Quarter teaspoon of mustard
1 small onion, finely chopped
2 teaspoons Worcester sauce
4oz. grated cheese
1-pint milk
1 tablespoon breadcrumbs

Method

Put the slices of bread and butter into a greased dish. Beat the eggs with seasonings and add the onion, Worcester sauce and most of the cheese. Stir in the milk and then pour the mixture into a dish. Leave to stand for about 10 minutes. Mix the remaining cheese and breadcrumbs together, sprinkle on the top of the pudding and bake in moderate oven until set. (4 servings) 350F or Gas Mark 4, cooking time is about 25-30 minutes.

Leigh cheese is another local cheese, specifically used for toasting, dating from at least the thirteenth century, from the dairy town of its name.

> The curd is broke down and when separated from the whey is put into a cheese vat and pressed very dry and after that broken very small by squeezing it with the hands. The new curd used is mixed with about half its quantity of yesterday's and which has been kept for that purpose and a part of this new curd is put by for tomorrow if it can be spared, if not all tomorrow's is put by to mix with new as convenience suits for the best cheese is always made with part old curds. Some mix the old and the new together after both have been worked very small others put the old curds in the middle of the cheese either of which ways will do very well as I have often noticed. When the curds have been thus mixed and well pressed and closed with the hands in a cheese vat till they become one solid lump it is put into a press.

It is this process which made it ideal for toasting.[17]

SWEET AND SAVOURY

According to the *Lancashire Evening Post* of 1932, Preston had 232 confectioners trading that year, serving around 120,000 inhabitants. The article suggests that the county had a sweet tooth, which it attributes to the dull life of the factory worker seeking stimulation.

Some readers may understandably associate rock with Blackpool, but its origins were slightly further up the coast. 'Dynamite' Dick Taylor, from Morecombe, should be credited as one of the earliest pioneers of rock, along with his invention of imprinting words in the rock itself. He inserted the letters TNT into his rock – Taylor's Noted Toffees – and had shops on the promenade and Pedder Street during the early part of the 1900s in Morecombe. But, he wasn't actually the first, as he admitted that someone else had being doing it at least twenty years before him in the town, in the 1890s. I found an article from 1891 noting the sale of 'Morecambe Rock' in Morecambe, 'in almost every shop and at the street corners'. It was described as 'great chunks of sweetmeat, pink and white as thick as a Field-Marshal's baton, pepper minted to the point of nausea'.[18] Also Dick Taylor allegedly carried out some heroic local act during the First World War, helping quell the fire in a munition's factory.[19] He was apparently still living in Mardale Avenue, Morecombe, by the mid-twentieth century. He made rock even more accessible with various flavours and colours, allowing him an assumed provenance for this sticky treat.

That most unmistakable of wondrous gelatine creations, the Jelly Baby was invented in Nelson, Lancashire, in the factory of sweet manufacturer Thomas Fryer. Born in Barrowford in 1841, he opened his first sweet shop at the age twenty-three, and by

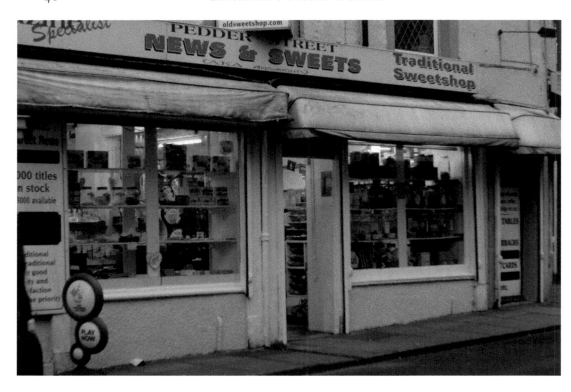

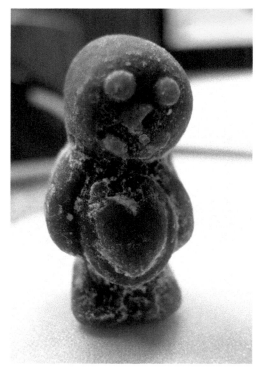

Above: Pedder Street, Morecambe. Original location of 'Dynamite Dick's' Morecambe rock shop. (© Nick Kay)

Left: Jelly Baby, invented in Nelson.

1871 he had four employees and was based in his original premises at Colne Road. As his reputation grew Fryer moved into the large Victory Works, where he also created his brand of cough lozenges, 'Victory V'. It was an Austrian immigrant working for the company, named Herr Steinbeck, who when asked to create a new jelly mould shaped like bears, made instead what resembled a baby – and that was that. Christened 'unclaimed babies', in an age of dark humour and a time when numerous babies were abandoned on doorsteps it was probably quite fitting. By the 1950s the world couldn't get enough of them and the 300-strong team of employees worked around the clock to manufacture, pack and distribute these now newly christened 'Jelly Babies', possibly a consequence of another manufacturer of the same confection based in London, who named them so. During the 1960s, Fryer and Co. were bought up by Scribbans-Kemp Ltd but was eventually closed and demolished in the 1980s.

Jelly Babies would have been a luxury treat in Lancashire at a time of industrial fatigue. They were sent to soldiers on the front line during the two World Wars and were voted the nation's sixth favourite sweet in 2009 by way of a Marks and Spencer poll. Bassetts, now Maynards Bassetts, began mass-producing them in 1918 and continue to keep the original concept of the Fryer product alive for us all to enjoy.[20]

Around the same time another popular sweet was being developed just down the road in Wigan, one with a minty, creamy taste and texture. Uncle Joe's Mint Balls were manufactured from 1898, hand cooked on open fires with the promise to 'keep you all aglow'. Ellen Seddon created Uncle Joe's Mint Balls, selling them from her husband, William Santus', fruit and vegetable stall and sales were so successful that they set up a partnership business in the confection trade. The name was patented in the 1930s and has since become an internationally recognised product that continues to reinvent itself in today's competitive markets.[21]

Stockley's Sweets, who produce their confectionery in Blackburn, are over one hundred years old and perhaps best known as the originators of Coltsfoot Rock, flavoured with extract from the coltsfoot daisy – as opposed to the hoof of a horse! Stockley's was also the home of the world's largest pear drop, now on display at Oswaldtwistle Mills shopping village.

The county's love of sweet-toothed inventions does not stop at confection. Iconic Hartley's Jam was founded by Sir William Pickles Hartley, whose family were thought to have descended from Huguenots. He was born in Colne where he ran a grocer's shop in the 1870s. Legend has it that due to an anticipated batch of jam not being delivered, Hartley was forced to make it himself. The business quickly expanded on the back of his talents and transferred to Liverpool to be closer to the docks where sugar was shipped in directly from the Caribbean. An industrial 'village' with over seventy workers' cottages and jam-themed street names was built, including redcurrant court and cherry row. Sadly, Hartley's was bought up by Premier Foods, then Hain Daniels Group, and is now manufactured in Cambridgeshire. The original village remains and has been granted Conservation Area status.

Another gentleman of French origin living and working in Manchester, Gabriel Hugon is the brainchild behind shredded suet. While watching his wife laboriously chopping suet in the kitchen one day, he decided to find a way to shred it on a large

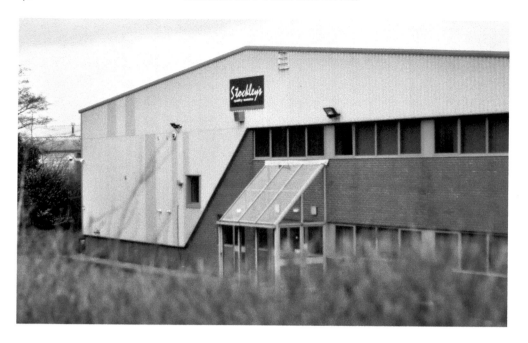

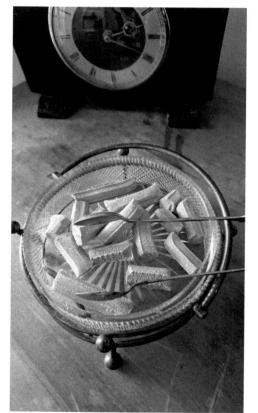

Above: Stockley's factory. (© Nick Kay)

Left: Coltsfoot Rock from Stockley's. (© Emma Kay)

scale for convenience. He abandoned his engraving business in 1893 and established a factory where beef fat was clarified and then grated before being packaged and transported all around the country.[22]

The name Atora was derived from *toro*, the Spanish word for bull. The company lost its independence to Rank Hovis McDougall in the 1960s, which in turn became Premier Foods.

Another kitchen cupboard staple was propelled into society in 1844, when Cartmel-born George Borwick launched his baking powder in London, which swiftly received royal patronage and an annual return of around £13,000 throughout the mid-1800s. His products were also patronised by the British Navy and Army – impressive for a simple mix of tartaric acid, soda, ground rice and a smidgeon of wheat.[23]

A humble product which has retained archetypal status was created by Louis Moore who worked in the meat trade throughout the later 1800s in Linacre Road, Liverpool, in the district of Litherland, Merseyside, formerly Lancashire. By 1920, together with his sons George and Alfred, the Richmond Sausage Company had become a national sought-after brand. The Moore family named the company after a Methodist training college in London and originally launched their products in South Wales.[24] Today the company is owned by the Kerry Group and no longer sports the original, slightly disturbing, logo of a jaunty pig carrying a sausage on a fork over its shoulder. But their products remain firm favourites in the British market along with another family brand, Warburtons, who now apply the Chorleywood method of bread making, where bread is mixed rapidly and mechanically, using numerous additives to manufacture products quicker and increase shelf life. It is also the largest family-owned bakery in the country. Originally Ellen and Thomas's grocery store located in Bow Street, Bolton, which is now nothing more than an industrial area of the town, with only half of Bow Street remaining, was in decline by 1876. To help boost sales Ellen Warburton began baking loaves and cakes daily. Popularity increased steadily and various family members were recruited to assist with the business. The rest is bread giant history.

Perhaps Holland's Pies once baked Lancashire or Collier's Foot, a pasty in the shape of a trotter, supposedly once eaten by local miners and farmers. Both recipe writers Dorothy Hartley and Gladys Mann mention the dish, but I can find no reference to them prior to their writings. Or Westhoughton pasties, which were large, regional, flat pork pasties enjoyed at 'Keaw Yed', meaning cow's head, Wakes. They were named after the local legend of a farmer who thought the best way to free one of his cows caught with its head in a gate was to remove its head.[25]

Holland's Pies were made famous by apprentice Richard Holland, who joined an existing confectioner's in Haslingden in the 1860s, eventually marrying one of the owners and re-christening the business as Holland's. Several generations of the same family continued to sustain the popularity of the bakery and expand its products. By the end of the 1920s a Holland's van met the increasing demand for the numerous deliveries in and around Haslingden and the outgrown premises moved to Baxenden. Just before the Second World War, one van was replaced by twenty and the fleet delivered the firm's most popular products, pies, to chip shops all over the region.

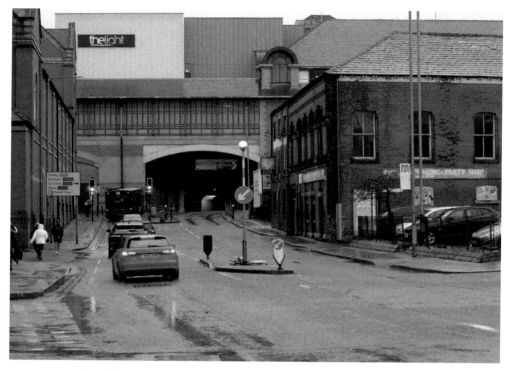

Original site of Warburtons bakery, Bow Street, Bolton. (© Nick Kay)

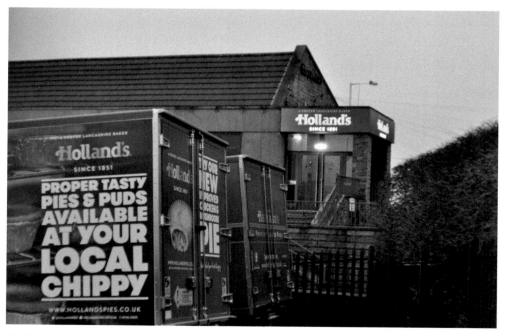

Holland's Pies factory premises. (© Nick Kay)

Following the war Holland's was bought by an outside company and then taken over by Pork Farms in the 1970s, before current ownership of the 2 Sisters Food Group took place in the earlier part of this century.

Holland's Pies continues to reinvent itself and stay current with trends, including a wide range of contemporary vegetarian and vegan products.

Lancashire Sauce is a unique product still made by Entwistle's. It is a mildly spiced liquid seasoning to add to soups, gravies, curries and all manner of other dishes.

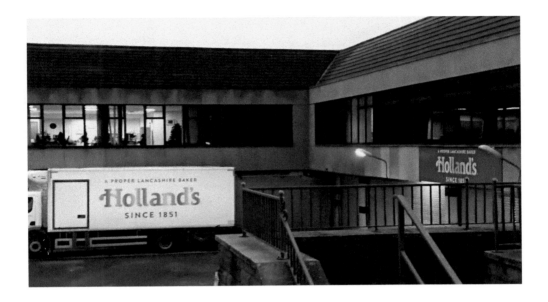

Above: Holland's Pies factory premises. (© Emma Kay)

Right: Lancashire Sauce. (© Emma Kay)

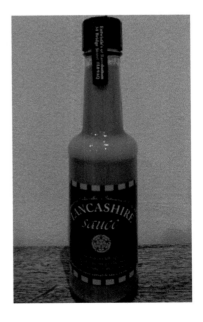

The earliest record I can find for it is 1851, when it was manufactured by Broome's, who appear to be the most prolific early makers of this local ambrosia, together with Mackrell's and Picton and Hatton. A recipe was published for Lancashire Sauce in a 1914 edition of *Pharmaceutical Formulas*:

> Table-salt, bruised capsicum, bruised pimento, bruised cinnamon, bruised cloves, bruised mace, bruised coriander, treacle, vinegar. Boil for half an hour, strain and add Indian soy and walnut ketchup. Keep in a warm place for a day and strain through a hair sieve.[26]

CAKES AND BISCUITS

From Sarah Nelson's still thriving legacy of the famous Grasmere recipe, to the bakers of Ormskirk, gingerbread has a long association with the county. Sally Woods was one of the best known of the Gingerbread Ladies of Ormskirk, a group of local women whose mothers and grandmothers had been in the gingerbread business before them, making it in their back kitchens and selling it on the streets of this northern industrial town. As the centuries rolled by, they went from meeting the stagecoaches as they pulled into the old Talbot Inn, to engaging with the passengers alighting at Ormskirk's railway station. One regular passenger who would have the train stop at Ormskirk en route to Scotland was King Edward VII, who bought gingerbread in abundance from Sarah Fyles, descended from a long line of local gingerbread sellers. She eventually

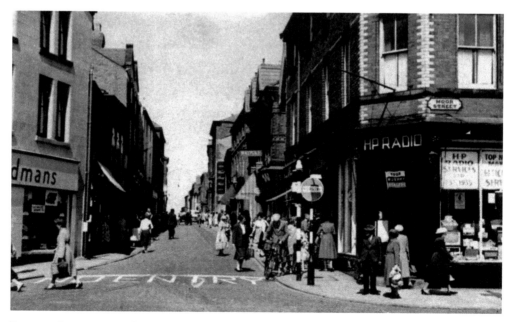

Burscough Street, Ormskirk. (Courtesy of Mark Crombie)

had the gingerbread wrapped and stamped with the phrase 'Established 1732, Fyles's celebrated Old Original Ormskirk Gingerbread, as patronized by His Majesty King Edward VII, Prince and Princess of Wales, T.R.H. The Duke and Duchess of Teck and the Nobility'.

All the sellers had their own unique characteristics and selling pitches, but Sally Woods had a reputation that far exceeded those before and after her. It is said that during her funeral, a prominent man of the town was heard to say, 'There goes a woman who was frightened of neither man, woman nor beast.' Her grandson John Neville recalled how she carried her basket of freshly baked gingerbread on one arm, with her pet gander waddling behind her. The gingerbread mix was made in the Woods' kitchen, before being taken to the communal ovens down a narrow passage called 'The Monkey's Nest'. Gingerbread men and donkeys with currants for eyes were some of the best known.

Soroptimist International, the national volunteer service for women, printed a Christmas card in 1958 depicting an old picture of hawker Esther Catterall wearing a feather bonnet and shawl, selling her gingerbread. Inside the card was printed an original recipe for Ormskirk gingerbread:

Ingredients: 2 ½ lbs flour, 1 lb brown sugar, ½ lb black treacle, 3ozs candied peel, 1 lb butter, ½ lb syrup, 1 teaspoon ground ginger, 1 wine glass of rum.

Method: Rub butter into flour and add ground ginger and brown sugar. Shred candied peel fine and mix dry ingredients thoroughly before adding syrup and treacle. This mixture becomes a stiff dough. Add the rum and continue to stir until all the ingredients are thoroughly mixed. Leave overnight, preferably in a warm room.

Next morning roll out to the thickness of an average biscuit, then cut into biscuits about the size of the top of a tumbler, using up the dough, by re-rolling and cutting.

Bake in a moderately hot oven until a rich brown and allow to cool. Store in air-tight tin to retain crispness.[27]

It seems that age-old talent for baking biscuits and cakes in the county continued. In 1911 the largest group of employees working in the food and drink sector in Lancashire were those who worked in bread and biscuit manufacture, some 19,000 in total.[28] Parkinson's Biscuits Ltd, based in Wesham since 1884 (actually called Phoenix Bakery), boasted the latest equipment for modern biscuit manufacture in 1957,[29] and Jacob's actually created a special biscuit for Lancashire in 1928 – Jacob's Lancashire Crackers.

One of the most well-known of brands that continues to manufacture some of Britain's best-loved snacks is Fox's Biscuits. Based in Yorkshire, Staffordshire and the small historic Lancashire town of Kirkham, the company hails from a heritage of brandy snap production in the mid-1800s, which grew and diversified into F. E. Fox & Co., named after Fred Ellis Fox.

It would be another local manufacturer that would become the second largest biscuit company in the UK. Bee Bee Biscuits started life as the Blackpool Biscuit

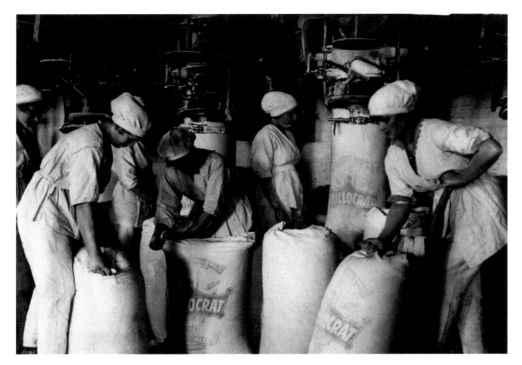

Female millers in Lancashire, 1914, packing flour. (Courtesy of UBC Library)

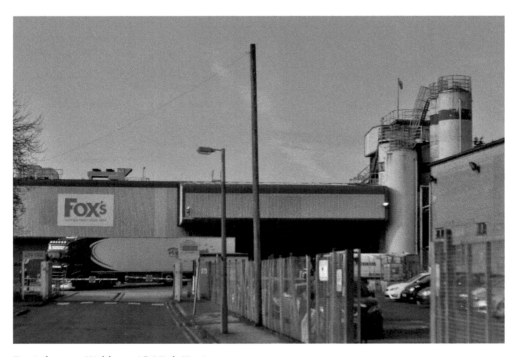

Fox's factory, Kirkham. (© Nick Kay)

Company in 1922, selling brandy snaps and Shrewsbury biscuits. London-based Lesme acquired control of the company in the 1930s, creating a North/South enterprise. A new factory was erected in Devonshire Road, Blackpool and Bee Bee became one of the pioneers of pre-packed biscuits. Later known as Symbol Biscuits owned by Lyons, the company manufactured around forty varieties of sweet and savoury biscuits sold under the distinguished lion's head logo. Maryland Cookies were introduced in the 1950s and with the addition of a Viennese whirl plant in the 1970s revenues continued to increase. The company was briefly rechristened Lyons Biscuits Ltd, before being sold to Hillsdown Holdings plc and becoming Burton's Foods Ltd.[30]

Cake makers are also a cherished part of Lancashire's culinary past. Thomas Clarke was known as the most famous simnel cake maker in Lancashire. His cakes were sold by Metcalfe Brothers, grocers based in St James's Street, Burnley. He was also a novelist and his cakes were exported as far as South Africa. His customers included the King of England and the Queen of Norway.[31] 'Simbling Sunday' was when large simnel cakes were sold mostly in the town of Bury and the shops stayed open for the whole day. They were eaten along with large draughts of mulled ale.[32] Another cake, which is often attributed to Lancashire but I believe has a much broader geographic provenance, extending to Somerset, is the courting cake – occasionally known as the Cumbrian courting cake or the Johnnie courting cake. I have even heard it called the Yorkshire Batley cake, which is more of a strawberry shortcake and like the recipe I acquired from Lancashire. It is probably a relative of the Victoria sponge sandwich. Certainly, references to the cake do not appear in the media until the early twentieth century and these are not exclusive to Lancashire. There is a much earlier reference

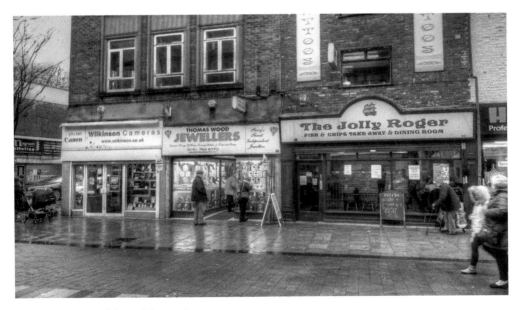

Bury. (Courtesy of Dave Morgan)

to a 'courting cake' baked by Abraham Lincoln's wife, Mary Todd, around 1840; however, the cake is a totally different version resembling a German almond bundt. This I believe was like the tonsure cakes baked on the Feast Day of Saint Anthony of Padua, as a symbol of love.

Much is written about the courting cake, as it was a cake baked by young Lancashire girls designed to woo their betrothed – something which was possibly prevalent around the 1920s. I have included a recipe here as it has so clearly been adopted by the county, although I would caution anyone into thinking that it was originally created in Lancashire. The following recipe comes once again from the parish of St Michael's Church, Weeton, a contribution of Kitty Garlick.

Grandma Kirby's Courting Cake

9 oz. Self-Raising Flour
4 ½ oz. Butter or Margarine
4 oz. Sugar
1 egg, whisked with a little milk

Method

Put flour, sugar and butter in a bowl. Mix together until like breadcrumbs. Add egg and milk to bind mixture together. (you may not need all the egg and milk). Divide mixture into two. Roll one out, put on a flat baking tray and spread with raspberry jam. Roll out the other half and place on top. Bake at 325 – 350 F. for approximately half an hour till golden brown. Sprinkle with castor sugar.

ECCLES AND CHORLEY CAKES

The Chorley variety, from its namesake town, is made using unsweetened shortcrust pastry, while the Eccles, from Manchester, is formed from flaky pastry with a sugar topping and originally served with cheese. Both are undoubtedly related to early 'fairings', which were small cakes often spiced or highly flavoured and bought at fairs and festivals to take home as gifts. Both are also said to be based on Banbury cakes; in fact, some published recipes for Eccles cakes, like that in *The Complete Practical Pastry Cook* by Gill Thompson (1889), suggest using the 'Banbury meat' as the basis for making the cake. It is difficult to establish which was first, although the Eccles cake has an older recorded provenance in literature to the Chorley, which is sometimes associated with the very similar 'sad cake', so called because it deflates in the middle during cooking, although these types of cakes required no rising. All were well known by the nineteenth century and James Birch is the baker typically credited with creating the Eccles variety, sometime towards the end of the 1700s. There is a famous tale of rivalry in the town, which led to the original cake maker erecting a board outside his premises, stating 'The old established Eccles cake-maker, never removed, nor never will do.'[33] Here is Elizabeth Raffald's recipe for sweet patties, possibly the inspiration for Birch's Eccles cake.

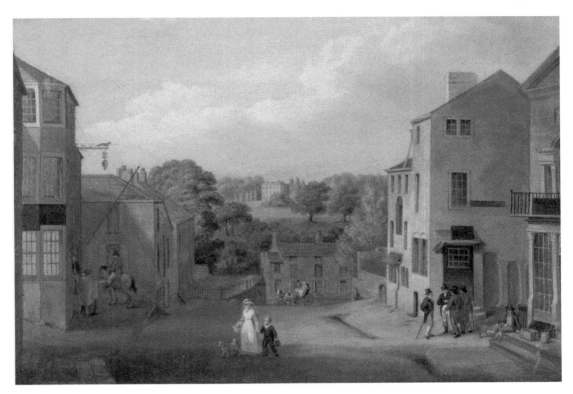

Chorley street scene, 1795. (Yale Collection)

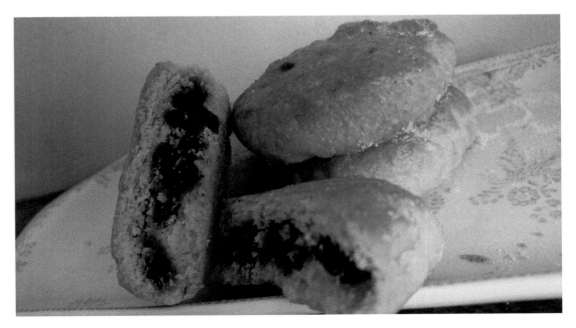

Chorley cakes. (© Emma Kay)

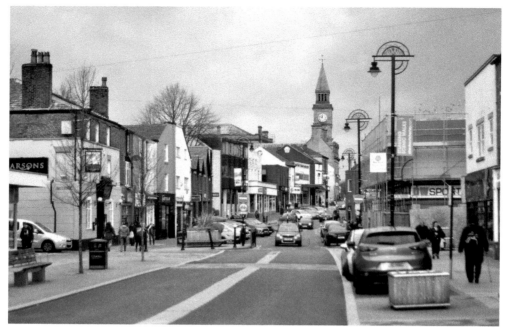

Chorley today. (© Nick Kay)

Sweet Patties

Take the meat of a boiled calf's foot, two large apples and one ounce of candied orange, chop them very small, grate half a nutmeg, mix them with the yolk of an egg, a spoonful of French brandy and a quarter of a pound of currants, clean washed and dried. Make a good puff paste, roll it in different shapes as the fried ones and fill them the same way. You may either bake or fry them. They are a pretty fine dish for supper.[34]

VICE AND VIMTO

The temperance movement was extremely prominent throughout the nineteenth and early twentieth centuries in Britain, with many groups mobilising against the consumption of alcohol. One of the key national advocates for temperance was Joseph Livesey, who was born in Walton-le-Dale. It is also said that the word 'teetotal' originated there, spoken during one of the temperance society meetings. *The Preston Temperance Advocate* was first published in 1834. It cost 1d and was one of the first publications relating to teetotalism in England.[35]

The most popular soft drink to come out of Lancashire must be Vimto. Originally created as an herbal tonic, John Noel Nichols launched his 'Vim and Vigour' Vimtonic in Manchester in 1908. Swiftly shortened to Vimto, the product was trademarked in 1912 as a medicine, before becoming registered as a beverage just a year later.

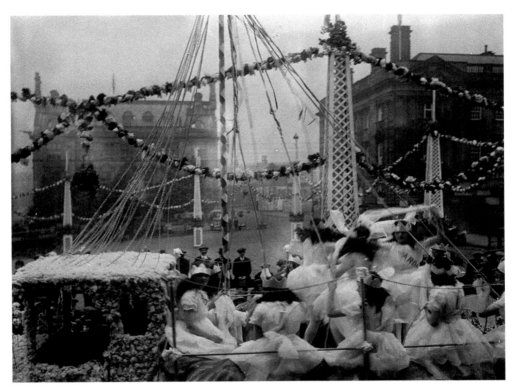

Preston Guild parade.

The drink was exported to India, where it became very popular, before taking on the Middle Eastern market just before the Second World War. Vimto took on many forms and was marketed in all kinds of ways: as a hot drink, a tonic and a cordial, before being rebranded in the 1960s as a canned drink, then more recently again as a sports drink, with no added sugar versions, squeezy novelty bottle versions and countless rebrands. It has found considerable popularity overseas among communities and religions who abstain from alcohol.[36]

Something a little harder was founded by Daniel Thwaites in the early 1800s, with Thwaites Brewery continuing to serve the county and surrounding UK out of Blackburn, although it now works collaboratively with Marston's. The brewery has a long legacy of family ownership and is often associated with the shire horse and horse-drawn deliveries, both of which it has reintroduced in recent years.

Whisky was also once commercially manufactured on a large scale in Manchester, Bolton and Liverpool and the county's illicit trade was rife in the Haslingden and Blackburn regions. Christened locally as 'whisky spinners', numerous remains of these moonshining enterprises have been unearthed. A complete underground whisky distillery was discovered carved into the rock behind a working farm near Calf Hey in 1857. The flue from the still was redirected into the main chimney for Bentley House, to disguise the additional smoke that was being generated. Right up until the end of the

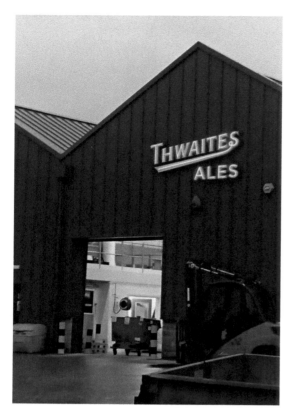

Left: Thwaites. (© Emma Kay)

Below: Haslingden at night. (© Nick Kay)

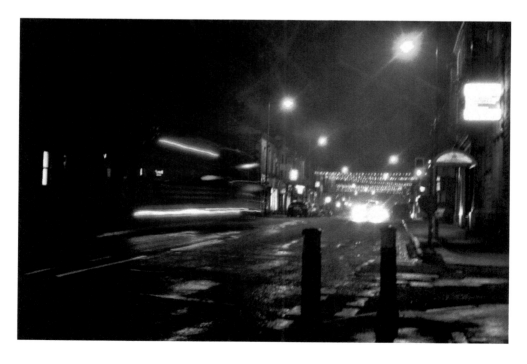

twentieth century there were parts of the community who, from childhood, still recalled sipping on 'the water of life of grane's'.[37] A ballad dedicated to a whisky spinner from the village of Grindleton in the Ribble Valley was published in the *Blackburn Standard* in 1888:

Near Grindleton fell owd Molly did dwell,
An became quite loved for her whisky O.
Spun far on the moor, away from her door,
Was owd Molly Peter's whisky O.
Now the gaugers come for mony a year.
They thowt foak geet summat stronger than beer;
An' ut last catch't Molly, when hoo thowt t'coast clear,
Wi a two gallon keg ov whisky O.[38]

BOOTHS

There is one place where you will find most of the quintessentially Lancastrian products discussed in this chapter, emerging during the same period. Booths stores were founded from 1847 by a young Edwin Henry Booth, who opened the first of his chain of shops in Blackpool. Booth wrote his autobiography in 1897 under the title of *Shadow and Sheen*, using the pseudonym Alec Gordon. Sadly, I have been unable to find an existing copy of this book, but a newspaper article written at the time of the stores' centenary celebrations provided a bit of background to Edwin's story. Born in Bury, he left home an unhappy child at the age of eleven, finding employment as an

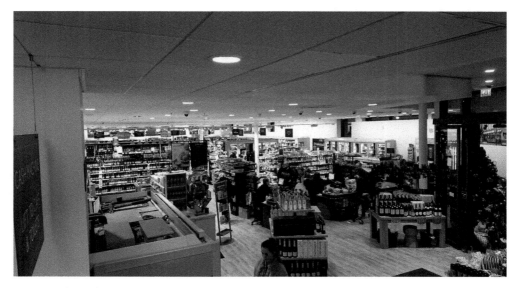

Interior of Booth's store. (© Emma Kay)

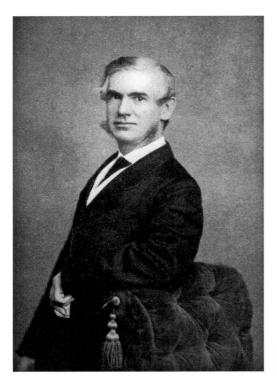

Edwin Henry Booth. (Courtesy of Preston Digital Archive)

errand boy for a tailor, earning 3 shillings a week, then became a grocer's assistant at nineteen. That same year he also paid his first visit to Blackpool, which he described as 'the rising watering place of Blackpool, to which the railway had just been extended' and swiftly opened a business there, followed by a second store in Chorley. The book details his love affair with Susannah Philips, the daughter of a corn miller from Colne, who he pursued for over three years before her father granted them permission to marry around 1855. The imposing architecture of Avenham Tower, Preston, now a listed building, was once the home of Edwin and his family. Booth ends the book with the following note:

> I have written my life hoping it may be an encouragement to every poor boy who may be similarly situated to persevere on the lines of truthfulness, industry and integrity. To all such I would say, strive to cultivate a feeling of self-respect and self-reliance, trust only in your own individual efforts, for I never knew anyone get on who was constantly leaning on others...[39]

Before he died, just two years after writing his story, Booth founded an orphanage in Preston, perhaps testament to his own childhood experiences. Today the twenty-eight-strong chain of stores remains a family-owned business and maintains an ethos of informality and personalised shopping. It is by far my favourite supermarket of choice – even more so now that I know a little more about its founder.

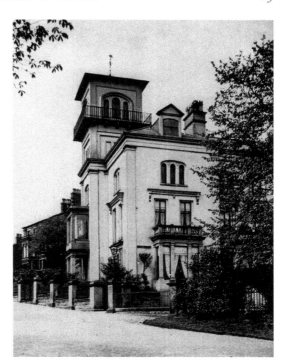

Right: Avenham Tower *c.* 1920. Home of
Edwin Booth. (Courtesy of Preston
Digital Archive)

Below: Orphans from St Annes-on-Sea
1943 Christms party, entertained by
the airmen at Warton. (Courtesy of
BAD-2 Association)

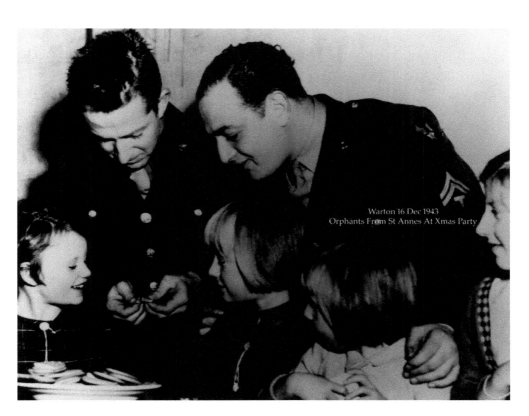

Warton 16 Dec 1943
Orphants From St Annes At Xmas Party

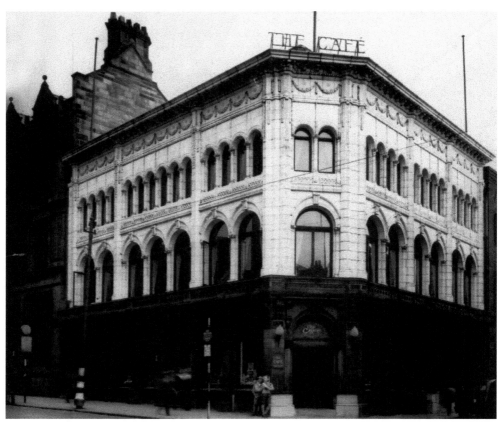

Booth's café and shop, Preston, *c.* 1935. (Courtesy of Preston Digital Archive)

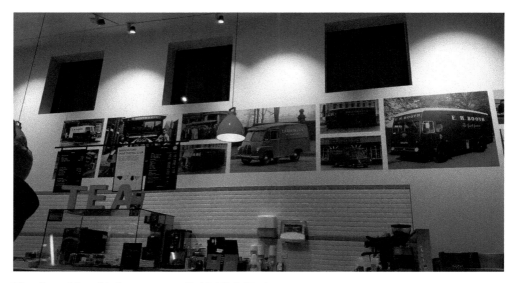

Timeline of Booth's from store café. (© Nick Kay)

4

Faitin and the Future

Thomas Thompson, a Lancashire writer and broadcaster from Bury, wrote a series of stories about East Lancashire. He described Sunday dinner just before the war:

> She had on Saturday had the luck to pick up at a Christian price a well upholstered ham 'pestil' [bone] which was a recognised basis for a good pan of steaming broth. There was pearl barley in it and 'pot yarbs' (herbs) and a 'beef bo' (beef pudding) for the head of the house, and a full range of suet dumplings to be well daubed with black treacle for the delectation of the 'childer' when they came from church.[1]

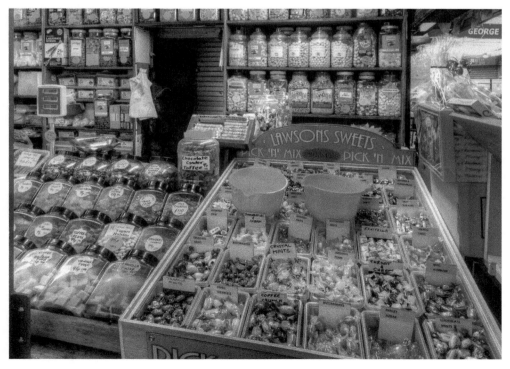

Lawsons Sweets, Bury, Est. 1955. (Courtesy of Dave Morton)

Many families in Lancashire, as with most counties then, grew vegetables and kept chickens during wartime, to supplement the rationing. Trainee nurses were fed marmite and peanut butter sandwiches, brought over from the US.

Orange peel was begged from local mill owners as a substitute for firelighters. Many people still remember Pimblett's bakery, whose pies were notorious, made distinctive with all the fresh black pepper they added to the fillings. The iconic St Helens firm collapsed in 2008 after three generations of family trading since 1921. People were prepared to travel significant distances to buy their products and Pimblett's became particularly well-known for their Christmas puddings. In 1998 they boasted almost 2,000 sales worldwide of this best-seller.[2] Greenhalgh's is another popular bakery founded in the mid-twentieth century and remains one of the largest employers in the Bolton area.

Preston would have been well-placed during the war with a busy port and good road links to the rest of Britain. Its rail station ran a free canteen for service personnel during the war. Sandwiches were mostly on offer, with a beetroot filling, which made the bread damp and pink.[3]

Pluck is a former term for cooking up sheep's heart, liver and lungs. One wartime evacuee told the story of an old pot constantly cooking on the open fire of the house she was staying in Bolton. It was referred to as 'dog's pluck', which conjures up all sorts of alarming images.[4] In Rochdale Mr Tweedale remembers eating horse and whale meat as a child growing up in the 1940s.[5]

During the war Liverpool docks was a prime target for German bombing raids and neighbouring northern towns and cities would have felt the brunt of this. The county is strewn with remnants of RAF training camps, pillboxes, air-raid shelters, decoy sites, airfield relics, ordnance factories and bomb sites. One of the most well-known

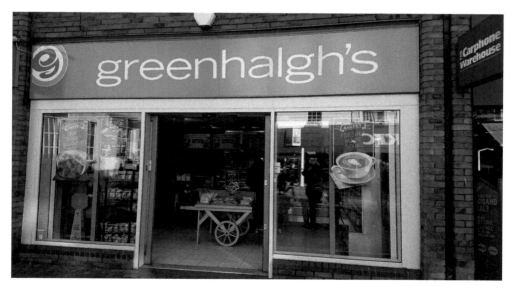

Greenhalgh's, Preston. (© Emma Kay)

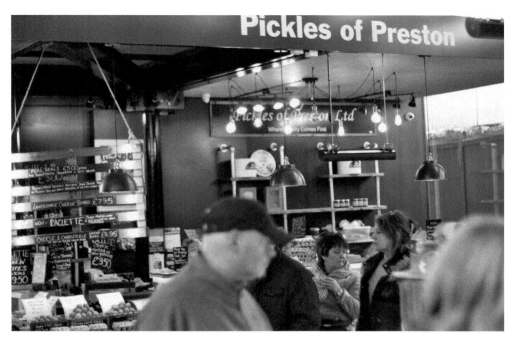

Preston indoor food market today. (© Nick Kay)

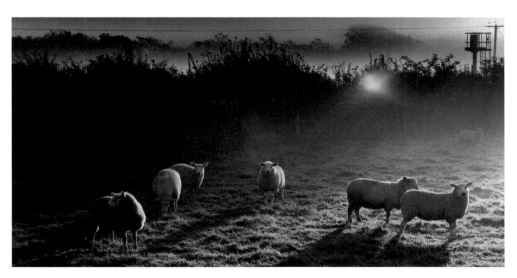

Lancashire sheep, Silverdale.

memorials to the war in Lancashire, in fact the entire UK, can be found in the Fylde village of Freckleton. At the rear of the church yard for Holy Trinity Church stands a Calgary cross on a two-tier step, flanked by two stones with the inscriptions of the names of the young children, teachers and civilians killed in the accident.

Many of the officers stationed at RAF Kirkham disliked the food that was served up and would go and seek breakfast or a cup of tea and a snack from the Sad Sack café in Freckleton. This was a hugely popular venue for both British and American airmen, based in a converted garage. The café's name was undoubtedly inspired by the American wartime cartoonist George Baker, who created the hugely popular comic strip *The Sad Sack*, about the misadventures of an army recruit. Twenty-year-old RAF Sergeant Walter Cannell was one of those café regulars and wrote a letter home declaring, 'there is this little café near here which sells lovely breakfasts. I often stay in bed and miss breakfast then get up and scrounge off after parade and go there.'[6]

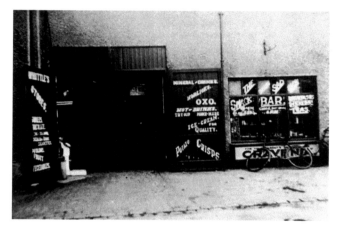

Left: Exterior of the Sad Sack café. (Courtesy of BAD-2 Association)

Below: Christmas and interior at the Sad Sack café. (Courtesy of BAD-2 Association)

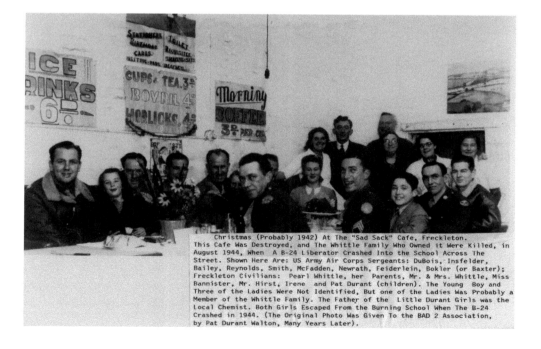

Christmas (Probably 1942) At The "Sad Sack" Cafe, Freckleton. This Cafe Was Destroyed, and The Whittle Family Who Owned it Were Killed, in August 1944, When A B-24 Liberator Crashed Into the School Across The Street. Shown Here Are: US Army Air Corps Sergeants: DuBois, Insfelder, Bailey, Reynolds, Smith, McFadden, Newrath, Feiderlein, Bokler (or Baxter); Freckleton Civilians: Pearl Whittle, her Parents, Mr. & Mrs. Whittle, Miss Bannister, Mr. Hirst, Irene and Pat Durant (children). The Young Boy and Three of the Ladies Were Not Identified, But one of the Ladies Was Probably a Member of the Whittle Family. The Father of the Little Durant Girls was the Local Chemist. Both Girls Escaped From the Burning School When The B-24 Crashed in 1944. (The Original Photo Was Given To the BAD 2 Association, by Pat Durant Walton, Many Years Later).

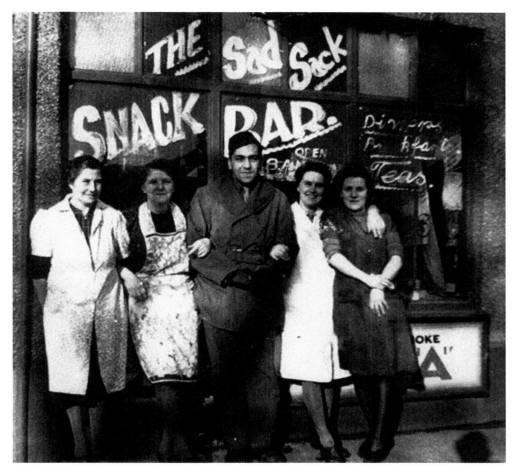

Sad Sack café staff with Sgt Joseph M. Elim in front of the premises. (Courtesy of Frank Nunez)

George Fisher, also based at the RAF station, recalled the following when interviewed in 2004:

'Sad Sack' café in Freckleton. On the morning of 23 August 1944, because I detested getting wet, I did not join four of my comrades at the cafe but stayed on camp. I can recall that as I made my way to the NAAFI in the gathering storm, there was a break in the clouds. In that moment, I saw a B-24 Liberator aircraft before it disappeared into the clouds. At that time, I was not aware that in fact there were two B-24s flying overhead in the storm, not having long before taken off from nearby Base Air Depot 2 to undertake air tests.

Not long after the sighting, one of the pilots, whilst approaching the base after a recall message, got into difficulties and as a result the aircraft crashed into the middle of the village with devastating results.

The Sad Sack café was one of the buildings which caught the full impact. Owners Mr and Mrs Whittle's daughter and four civilians were killed, along with seven USAAF personnel. Two RAF sergeant's aircrew and one a pilot were also killed. Five RAF aircrew died of injuries and five RAF personnel were rescued with very serious injuries.[7]

Down and across the road from the café, the young children of the village were having their morning lessons at Holy Trinity Primary School. Only three children from the infant classroom survived the crash; thirty-eight children and two teachers died. The total death toll following the Freckleton air disaster was sixty-one. It is thought to be one of the worst disasters to occur on British soil in the Second World War. Sergeant Walter Cannell was enjoying one of his much-loved breakfasts when the plane careered into the Sad Sack café. Rescued by American GIs, he would tragically be the last of the four British airmen to die from his injuries.[8]

The Ministry of Food ran a campaign in 1942 to encourage women from all over the country to meet in London and share cookery knowledge, tips and recipes. Mrs Taylor of Oldham was one of those women and the recipe she shared was for Lancashire hotpot.

Cooking time; 1 1/2 to 2 hours. Ingredients: lb. meat, a carrots, t onion or leek, if possible, 3 lbs. potatoes, ½ pint vegetable stock, 1 dessertspoonful fat from the meat or dripping, 1 dessertspoonful flour, pepper and salt. Quantity: Six helpings. Method: Cut up meat into small pieces and place in a fireproof dish or casserole. Add sliced carrots and onion or leek, and pepper and salt. Add half the potatoes. Instead of slicing potatoes crack off lumps with a knife. Place the fat from the meat or the dripping on top. Put in a moderate oven with lid on for half an hour. Take out, add stock, blend 1 dessertspoonful flour in a little water, pour into casserole. Add remainder of potatoes and sprinkle with salt and pepper. Cook in a moderate oven. Remove the lid for the last 20 minutes and cook until the potatoes are brown.[9]

Just as the Women's Institute came into their own during the war, the Mothers' Union remains intrinsic to many of the village communities of Lancashire. Members of the Freckleton and surrounding branches were very helpful with contributing recipes to this book, via the adept organisation skills of current local Mother's Union chairwoman and my mother-in-law Anne Kay. Recipes including Bardsley cake, provided by Dorothy Smith, offer an insight into this once very fashionable, now almost obsolete, fruit cake, originally from Oldham. Here is her recipe:

Bardsley Cake

½ lb Castor sugar
½ lb Margarine
¾ lb Self-raising flour
12 oz. Sultanas
6 oz Currants
1 oz Orange
2 oozes. Ground Almonds
4 Eggs

Method

Grate orange rind, soak fruit in orange juice. Cream butter and sugar, add eggs, then fruit, ground almonds, flour and orange rind. If too stiff add 2 tablespoons milk. Fill 8" cake tin. Bake for ½ hour 300F., 1 ½ hours 250F.

Right: Contemporary curry hotpots at Fazz's, Bolton. (© Emma Kay)

Below: Mothers' Union Service, 2019. (Courtesy of Anne Kay)

There were some seventy-six tripe shops in 1911 in Bolton alone and hundreds were still open across the county right up until the 1960s. As a result of the growth of intensive farming in the area, there are now none.[10] This edible lining of animal stomach is often associated with Lancashire, perhaps in part due to the local success of United Cattle Products Ltd (UCP), whose chain of shops and restaurants across the county dedicated to tripe would have made it both highly accessible and heavily promoted to consumers.

Here is a wartime recipe from 1940, published in the *Rochdale Observer*:

TRIPE AND ONIONS First prepare the tripe by blanching it that is putting it in a pan of cold water and bringing it closely to boiling point. The water should then be thrown away, and the tripe cut into neat oblong pieces. Peel three or four large onions

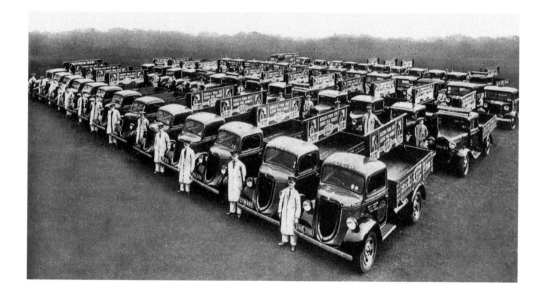

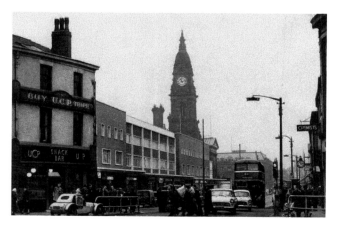

Above: United Cattle Products vehicles. (Courtesy of United Cattle Products.co.uk fansite)

Left: One of the original UCPs in Bolton. (Courtesy of United Cattle Products.co.uk fansite)

and cut them into slices. Put the tripe and onions into a saucepan or casserole with one pint of milk, and let it simmer slowly for at least two hours. Mix a dessertspoonful of flour to a paste with a little cold milk in which the tripe is cooking. Let it boil up and thicken, and then season to taste with pepper and salt. A few cloves added to the milk before simmering the tripe are an improvement if liked.[11]

Although the UCP petered out in the 1960s, numerous historically established food businesses continue to thrive in the county. Today, market gardening plays a significant role in Hesketh Bank and its surrounds, including Hundred End, Banks and Tarlton. A couple of the bigger-name suppliers include Wright Farm Produce and Croftpak Nurseries. In the past the area had a strong connection to celery cultivation and a drive around the area could end with a fascinating chat with local resident Janet Baxter, whose husband Alec was an extremely popular and dynamic figure in the community – charity worker, collector, sculptor, market gardener and one-time owner of Baxter beetroot. The whole area is a vast expanse of big skies and open fields producing a wealth of lettuces, cabbages and tomatoes.

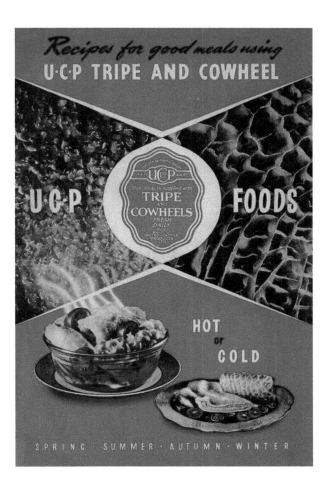

UCP recipe leaflet. (Courtesy of United Cattle Products.co.uk fansite)

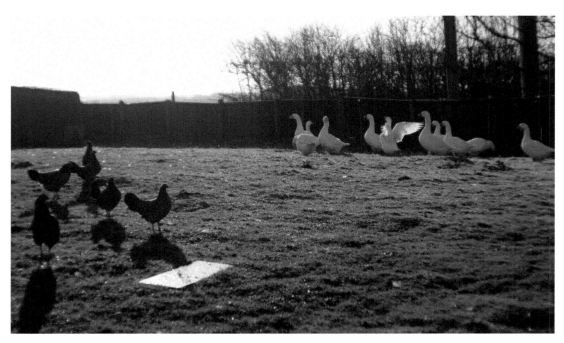

Geese and chickens at Banks. (© Nick Kay)

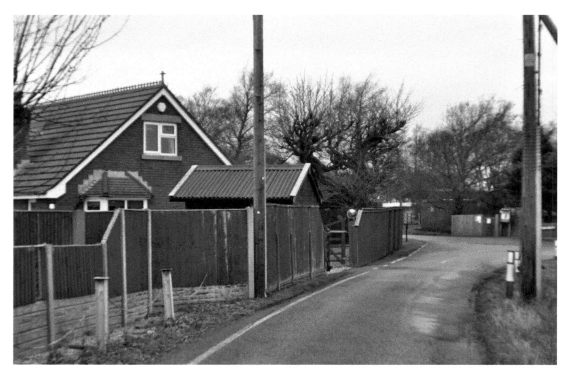

Location of the old rail station and celery junction at Hundred End. (© Nick Kay)

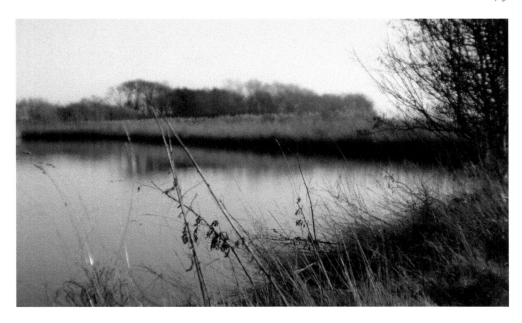

Above: Scenes from Banks near the home of Janet Baxter. (© Nick Kay)

Right: Baxter's beetroot sign belonging to Janet Baxter. (© Emma Kay)

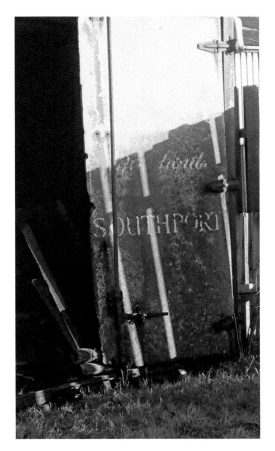

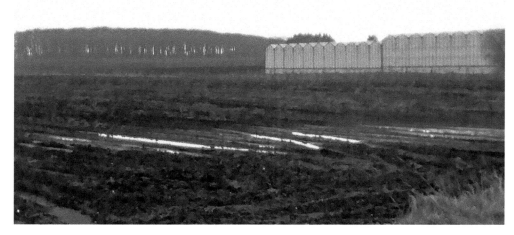

The market gardens of Hundred End. (© Emma Kay)

Garstang cheesemakers Dewlay have traded under the guiding hands of the Kenyon family since 1957 and their shop is an absolute joy to visit, while Proctor's Cheese have been operating out of the village of Chipping since the 1930s and J J Sandham make both traditional, goat, sheep and smoked cheeses with a history of manufacture spanning eighty years.

Third-generation cheesemaker Graham Kirkham still follows his grandmother's recipe and 'Mrs. Kirkham's Lancashire Cheese' is produced from the family's own dairy herd in Goosnargh. This same village is home to established national poulters Johnson and Swarbrick, who, along with the village itself, have a long heritage associated with the production of geese, ducks and chicken.

Once a town known for its thriving fishing industry, Fleetwood no longer produces anything on the scale (pardon the pun) that it once did. The one-time bustling docks, thriving fish market and huge railway station connecting the railway line to the pier are mere shadows of the past. However, My Fish Company continue to supply the town and far-reaching locations, restaurants and pubs with their daily service providing the freshest caught fish and shellfish. The age-old practice of shrimping, cockling and other shellfish hauls has also been integral to Morecambe Bay's coastal commercial history for centuries. Baxters, the proud owners of a Royal Warrant, have been potting shrimps in the area since 1799. Fish and chips are the stuff of legend in Lancashire, with many places on the coast from the traditional Seniors chain of shops and independent restaurants like Seafarers in Lytham St Annes to Blackpool's seafront Beach House Bistro and Bar, who offer a modern, fresh twist providing the highest quality of this classic favourite dish.

Local Herdwick sheep reared by fifth-generation farmer Ian Knight and his family continue to provide consumers with the finest lamb and mutton. Butcher's-like Beltin Good Beef have been based at Croasdale House Farm in Slaidburn since 1983.

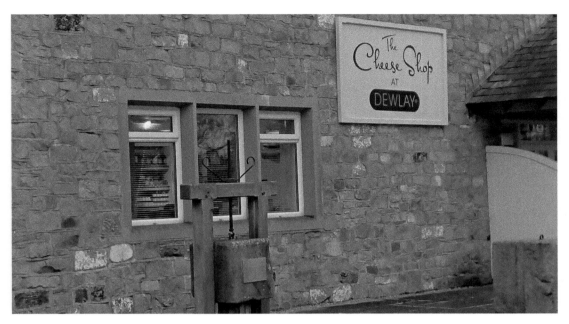

Dewlay cheese, Garstang. (© Emma Kay)

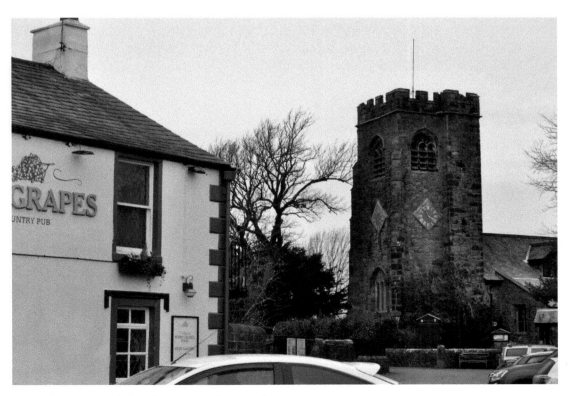

Village pub and church, Goosnargh. (© Nick Kay)

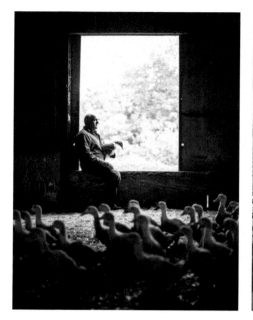 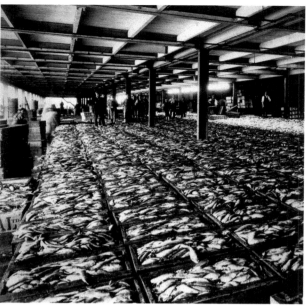

Above left: Johnson & Swarbrick poultry producers, Goosnargh. (© Johnson & Swarbrick)

Above right: Herrings for sale, Fleetwood fish market, 1910. (Courtesy of Fleetwood Museum)

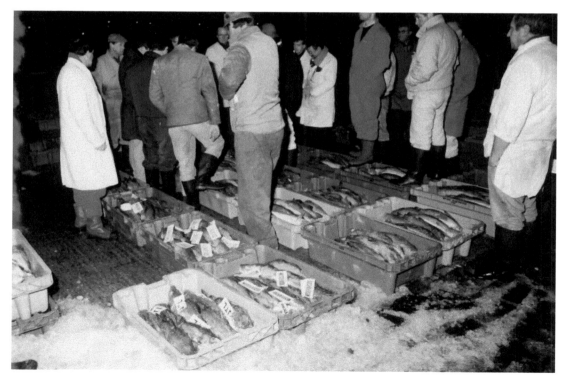

Fleetwood fish market in the twentieth century. (Courtesy of Fleetwood Museum)

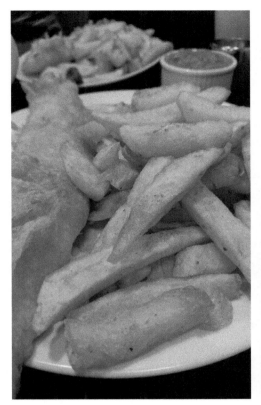

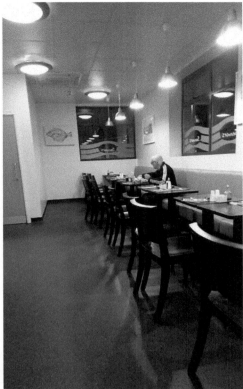

Above left: Fish and chips from Seniors. (© Emma Kay)

Above right: Seniors, Bispham. (© Emma Kay)

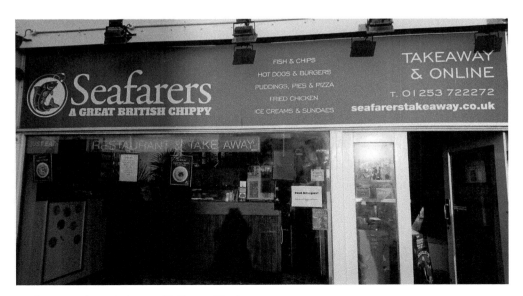

Seafarers, Lytham St Annes. (© Emma Kay)

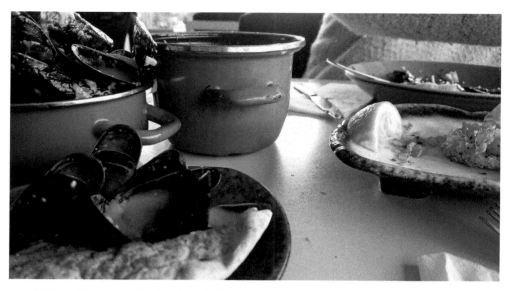

Beach House Bistro and Bar, Blackpool. (© Emma Kay)

Cowman's Famous Sausage Shop – butcher's for over 120 years – is in Clitheroe. The Robinson brothers' butcher's, established in 1906, is in Chipping and the family-run T. R. Snape and Sons butcher's shop is in the village of Freckleton, established in 1864, and I can testify they sell the best topside of beef I have ever tasted.

Gazegill Organics boasts a farming legacy of some five-hundred years and the Ashcroft family farm, comprising the Owd Barn Country Store and Tea Room in Ormskirk, has grown their cereal and arable crops for over two hundred years. Ormskirk is also where the historic potato farming Fiddler family now run their crisp empire, including locally patriotic flavours such as Lancashire Black Pudding, Lancashire Cheese and Onion and Lancashire Sauce. Huntapac is a fourth-generation, family-led business specialising in growing, packing and distributing vegetables and salads.

Victuals also have a heritage in the county from wine merchants D. Byrne & Co. who have been trading in the Ribble Valley area for over 130 years and the famous J. Atkinson & Co wholesale and retail coffee and tea traders, operating out of Lancaster since 1837. There exists a wealth of food and drink producers across Lancashire who have been successfully trading for several generations and longer from Holdens and Co. Ice cream makers in Edgworth with a legacy extending from 1929, who have adapted into a broader village shop serving the whole community. Bruccianis of Preston and Morecambe, two elegant vintage cafes, opened by Luigi Brucciani who allegedly walked from Italy to Scotland, together with his family in the late 1800s/early 1900s. Duerden's Confectionery of Burnley, Greenfields Dairy products, the Exchange Coffee Company, Lathams Bakery, Beeches Chocolates, Mrs. Dowson's ice cream, Wallings Ice-Cream and chocolate shop, The Ship Inn Freckleton along with a myriad of other ancient inns and taverns – many more that I regret I simply do not have the word count to include.

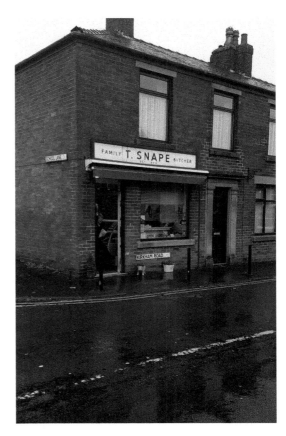

Right: T. R. Snape & Sons, butcher's, Freckleton. (© Nick Kay)

Below: Huntapac, Tarleton. (© Nick Kay)

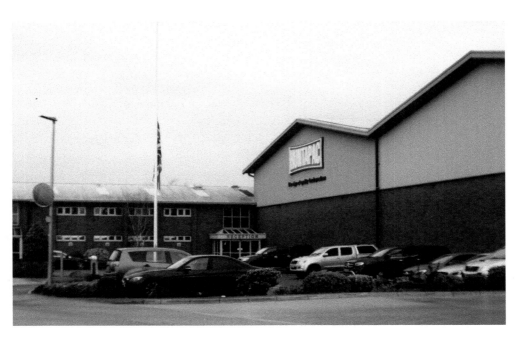

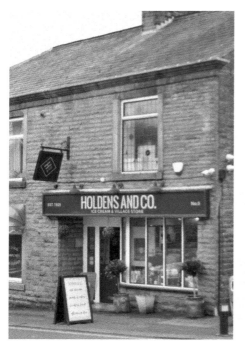 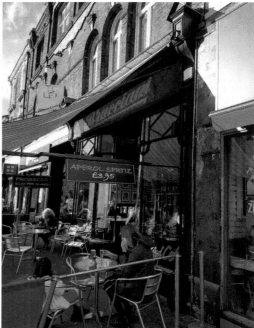

Above left: Holden's & Co., Edgeworth. (© Nick Kay)

Above right: Brucciani, Preston. (© Nick Kay)

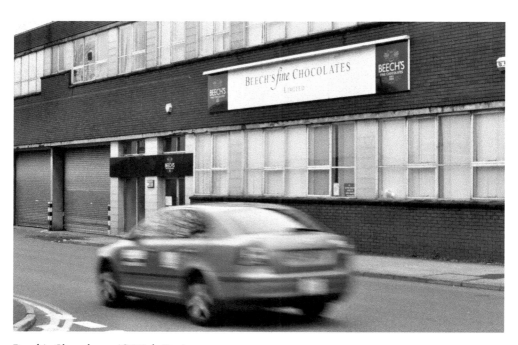

Beech's Chocolates. (© Nick Kay)

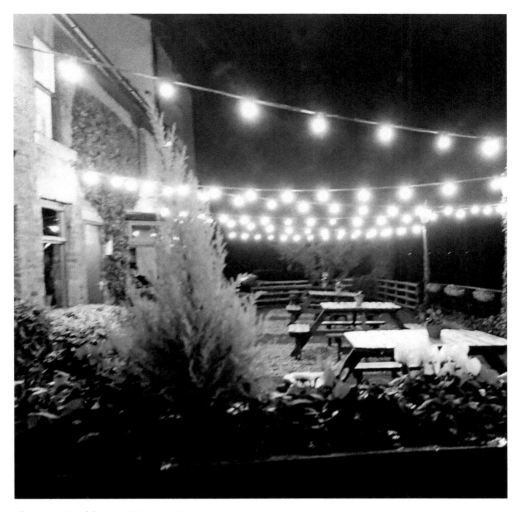

Ship Inn, Freckleton. (© Emma Kay)

There is now a contemporary breed of culinary entrepreneurs who maintain echoes of historical products with a modern approach.

Andrew Molyneux is one of a very few Formby asparagus growers. With such a short season and little suitable land available to grow this once highly prized product from nearby Liverpool is in danger of becoming obsolete. It was once supplied to all the large ocean liners embarking on transatlantic crossings. Gin is also a hugely popular local product, independently made by a selection of highly crafted distillers from the stunningly decadent and colourful Blackpool Rock Gin, combining two iconic British culinary favourites, small-scale, hand-made, cooper distilled Goosnargh Gin from the Forest of Bowland along with Bowland Distillery, Lytham Gin, Black Powder Gin, Burnley Batch Gin, Ribble Valley Gin and possibly the most quirky - Cuckoo Gin, inspired by the legendary Brindle cuckoo and located in the same village.

The cuckoo historically heralds the start of Spring and greedy villagers of old decided to trap their local cuckoo to stay all year round, sustaining successful harvests. The bird out foxed them and escaped, but each new baby born to the village is to this day known as a Brindle Cuckoo. Lytham Honey, Lancashire Farm yoghurts, Pennine Way Preserves, Stephenson's Dairy, Bowland Forest Eggs, The Real Lancashire Black Pudding Co., Dove Syke Cider, Cockerham Boers Farm goat meat, D&G Jolley's Potatoes, Chocolate Magic of Ormskirk, Butlers Farmhouse Cheeses, including Inglewhite Goats Cheese, Bowland Brewery, Lancaster Brewery, Lytham Brewery... The list goes on.

Lancashire County Council recently announced its new initiative, the *Two Zero: Food & Drink* programme, which seeks to develop Lancashire food and drink businesses. And so the culinary legacy continues.

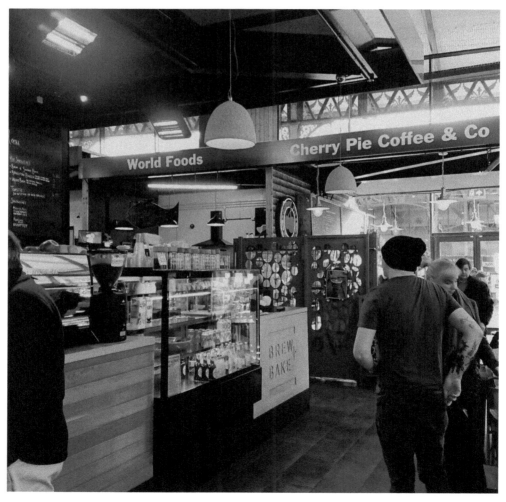

Preston indoor food hall. (© Nick Kay)

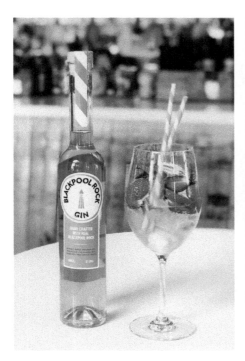

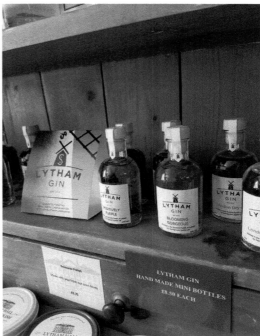

Above left: Blackpool Rock Gin.
(© Blackpool Rock Gin)

Above right: Lytham gin.
(© Nick Kay)

Right: Lytham honey. (© Nick Kay)

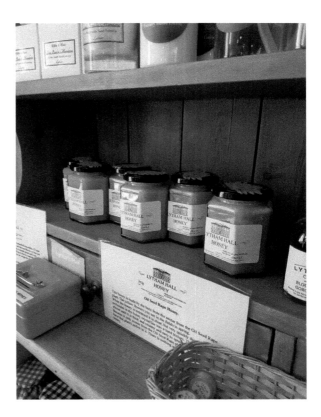

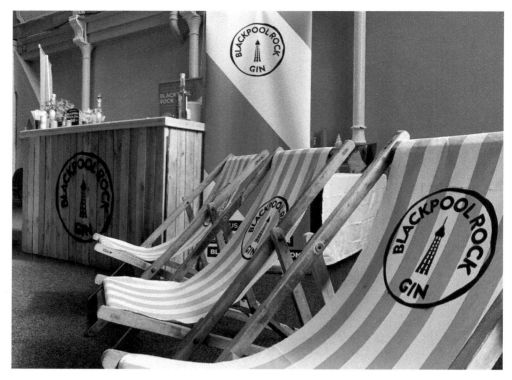

Blackpool Rock Gin chairs. (© Blackpool Rock Gin)

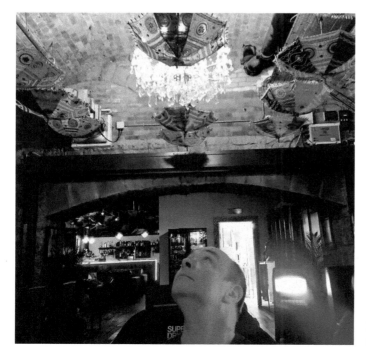

Fazz's, Bolton.
(© Emma Kay)

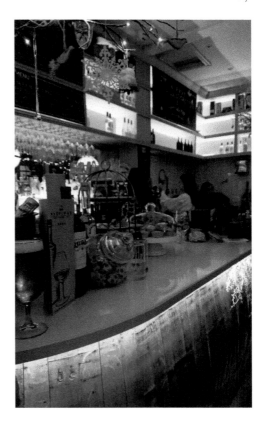

Right: Barrique wine shop, deli and bar, Lytham St Annes. (© Emma Kay)

Below: Goosnargh crossroads. (© Johnson & Swarbrick)

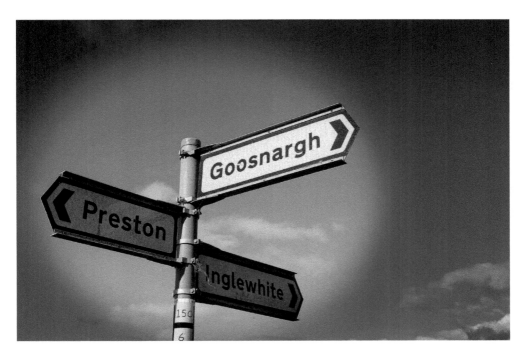

Notes

1. OWD LANCASHIRE

1. Harland, J., Wilkinson, T. T., *Lancashire Folklore* (Kessinger Publishing, 2003), p.227
2. British Newspaper Library, *Bolton Chronicle* (Saturday 10 Aug 1850)
3. Woolley, H., *The Queen-like Closet; or, Rich cabinet stored with all manner of rare receipts for preserving, candying & cookery. Very pleasant and beneficial to all ingenious persons of the female sex* (1670), p.272
4. Hughes, G., *The Lost Foods of England* (Denver House, Derbyshire, 2017), p.128
5. The Folk-Song Society, in *Local Gleanings Relating to Lancashire and Cheshire: Volume. 1-2* (London, 1875–78)
6. British Newspaper Library, *Sheffield Independent* (Saturday 5 Dec 1829)
7. Brockett, J. T., *A Glossary of Northern Country Words* (Newcastle, 1825), p.176
8. Barton, B. T., *History of the borough of Bury and Neighbourhood*, in The County of Lancaster (Wardleworth, Bury, 1874), p.109.
9. British Newspaper Library, *Dundee Evening Telegraph* (Thursday 19 April 1928)
10. Harland, J., Wilkinson, T. T., *Lancashire Legends, Traditions, Pageants, Sports, &c.* (Routledge, London and Manchester, 1873), p.240.
11. Morris, R. (ed.), *Liber Cure Cocorum* (A. Asher & Co., Berlin, 1862)
12. Morris, R. (ed.), *Liber Cure Cocorum* (A. Asher & Co., Berlin, 1862
13. Abram, A., *A History of Blackburn: Town and Parish* (Heritage Publications, 2014), p.585
14. Ashmore, O., *Household Inventories of the Lancashire Gentry 1550-1700* (Historic Society of Lancashire And Cheshire, Liverpool, 1958) p.89-9
15. Ashmore, O., *Household Inventories of the Lancashire Gentry 1550-1700* (Historic Society of Lancashire And Cheshire, Liverpool, 1958) p.92-97
16. Ashmore, O., *Household Inventories of the Lancashire Gentry 1550-1700* (Historic Society of Lancashire And Cheshire, Liverpool, 1958) p.92
17. Newbery, J., *A Pocket Dictionary: Or complete English Expositor* (the Bible and Sun in St Paul's churchyard, 1758)
18. Warner, R., *Ancient Cookery [Arundel Collection 334]* (London, 1791)
19. MacDonell, A., (ed.), *The closet of Sir Kenelm Digby Knight Opened* (Philip Lee Warner, London, 1669, 1910), p.149

20. Chaucer, G., *The Miller's Prologue and Tale* (Cambridge University Press, Cambridge, 2016), p.27.

21. Roud, S., *The English Year, Steve Roud* (Penguin, London, 2006)

22. British Newspaper Library, *Preston Herald* (Saturday 10 March 1888)

23. MacDonell, A., (ed.), *The closet of Sir Kenelm Digby Knight Opened* (Philip Lee Warner, London, 1669, 1910), p.108.

24. Hartley, D., *Food in England: A Complete Guide to the Food that Makes us Who We Are* (Piatkus, 2009), p.190

25. Carrick, J. C., *Wycliffe and the Lollards* (C. Scribner's & Sons, New York, 1908), p.173

26. Partington, S. W., *The Danes in Lancashire and Yorkshire* (Sherratt & Hughes, London and Manchester, 1909), p.66

2. UM STUARTS AND GEORGES

1. Stout, W., *Autobiography of William Stout, of Lancaster, wholesale and retail grocer and ironmonger, a member of the society of friends. A.D 1665-1752* (Simpkin & Marshall, London, 1851)

2. Abram, A., *A History of Blackburn: Town and Parish* (Heritage Publications, 2014), p.126

3. Iredale, D. A., *The Rise and Fall of The Marshalls of Northwich, 1720-1917* (1966), p.60.

4. British Newspaper Library, *Liverpool Echo* (Tuesday 28 July 1959)

5. Andrews, C., *The Country Cooking of Ireland* (Chronicle Books, California, 2009), p.299

6. British Newspaper Library, *Vote* (Friday 28 July, 1933)

7. Raffald, E., *The Experienced English Housekeeper* (Davies and Booth, Leeds, 1818), p.9-10

8. 'Ordinary's Account, 16 June 1693'. Ref: OA16930616 *Proceedings of the Old Bailey.* https://www.oldbaileyonline.org/browse.jsp?id=OA16930616& div=OA16930616&terms=lancashire#highlight Accessed, 03/12/2019

9. 'Ordinary's Account, 24 May 1695'. Ref: OA16950524 *Proceedings of the Old Bailey.* https://www.oldbaileyonline.org/browse.jsp?id=OA16950524& div=OA16950524&terms=lancashire#highlight Accessed, 03/12/2019

10. 'Ordinary's Account, 23 April 1697'. Ref: OA16970423. *Proceedings of the Old Bailey.* https://www.oldbaileyonline.org/browse.jsp?id=OA16970423& div=OA16970423&terms=lancashire#highlight Accessed, 03/12/2019

11. Clayton, J. A., *The Lancashire Witch Conspiracy: Histories and New Discoveries of the Pendle Witch Trials* (Barrowford Press, 2007), p.187

12. Poole, R., (ed.), *The Lancashire Witches: Histories and Stories*, (Manchester University Press, Manchester and New York, 2002), p.77

13. Tonge, M., *The Lancashire Witches: 1612 and 1634* (Trans. Historical Society of Lancashire and Cheshire, Volume 83, 1931), p.158

14. 'Forest of Pendle in the Seventeenth Century, Part Two', p.79. https://www.hslc. org.uk/wp-content/uploads/2017/05/115-5-Brigg.pdf (Accessed 4/01/2020

15. Bradley, R., *The Country Housewife and Lady's Director in the Management of a House, and the Delights and Profits of a Farm* (D. Browne and T. Woodman, London, 1732)

16. Sanderson, W., *Songs and Miscellaneous Poems* (I. Nevatt, Lancashire, 1849), p.87

17. Roeder, C., 'Rise and Growth of Blackpool', *The Historic Society of Lancashire and Cheshire* 1902, Manchester. P.1https://www.hslc.org.uk/wp-content/uploads/2017/11/54-2-Roeder.pdf (Accessed 09/02/2020)

18. Stout, W., *Autobiography of William Stout, of Lancaster, wholesale and retail grocer and ironmonger, a member of the society of friends. A.D 1665-1752* (Simpkin & Marshall, London, 1851), p.113

19. Roeder, C., 'Rise and Growth of Blackpool', *The Historic Society of Lancashire and Cheshire* 1902, Manchester. P.1 https://www.hslc.org.uk/wp-content/uploads/2017/11/54-2-Roeder.pdf (Accessed 09/02/2020)

20. Nodal, J., H., Milner, G., *A Glossary of Lancashire Dialect* (Alexander Ireland & Co., Manchester and London, 1875), p.262

21. Waugh, E., *Sketches: Rochdale to Blackstone Edge*, (John Heywood, London), p. 128

22. Bradley, R., *The Country Housewife and Lady's Director in the Management of a House, and the Delights and Profits of a Farm* (D. Browne and T. Woodman, London, 1732)

23. Axon, E., *Sunday in Lancashire and Cheshire* (1881), p.63/64

24. Miller, Gary *External Influences on English: From its beginnings to the Renaissance* (Oxford University Press, Oxford, 2012)

3. BRASS, BOOTHS AND BOATS

1. Fowler, A., *Lancashire cotton operatives and work, 1900-1950: A Social History of Lancashire Cotton Operatives in the Twentieth century* (Routledge, Oxford, 2018)

2. *The condition and treatment of the children employed in the mines and collieries of the United Kingdom 1842. Commissioners for inquiring into the employment and condition of children in mines and manufactories* (William Strange, London), p.23

3. Waugh, E., *Home-life of the Lancashire Factory Folk During the Cotton Famine* (Manchester Examiner and Times, Manchester, 1862)

4. US Newspapers Library of Congress, *The Herald News* (16 July 2010)

5. *City Documents 1921* (Fall River, Massachusetts, 1921), p.720

6. British Newspaper Library, *Lancashire Evening Post* (Wednesday 29 September 1937)

7. 'Fleetwood and Fishing: Songs of the Trawling Trade' https://mudcat.org/thread.cfm?threadid=137101 (Accessed,20/01/2020)

8. Millers, N., *The Lancashire Nobby* (Amberley, Gloucestershire, 2009)

9. Carter, G, G., *Red Charger: A Trip on the Arctic Fishing Grounds* (Constable, 1950), p.128-129

10. Landless, V., *Preesall Salt Mines* British Mining No.11 (Northern Mine Research Society, 1979), p.38-43
11. Ibid.
12. British Newspaper Library, *Liverpool Echo* (Saturday 26 August 1933)
13. Webb, A., *Food Britannia* (Random House, London, 2012)
14. British Newspaper Library, *Manchester Times* (Friday 08 July 1892)
15. British Newspaper Library, *Preston Chronicle* (Saturday 25 February 1893)
16. Humphrey Marshall, W., *A Review of the Reports to the Board of Agriculture, from the Northern Dept* (Thomas Wilson and Son, London, 1808), p.321
17. British Newspaper Library, *Daily Telegraph & Courier* (Friday 04 Sep 1891)
18. British Newspaper Library, *Daily Mirror* (Monday 20 April 1964)
19. Charlie Smith, 'Sweet shop favourite born in Lancashire', *Lancashire Post*, 2018, https://www.lep.co.uk/lifestyle/nostalgia/sweet-shop-favourite-born-in-lancashire-1-9199299 (Accessed 05/02/2020)
20. 'Uncle Joe's History', *Uncle Joe's Mint Balls*, https://uncle-joes.com/ (Accessed 02/03/2020)
21. *The Family of Catharine Donnix formerly Gibson* (1817-1887, http://adamantane.madasafish.com/GibsonCatharine.html, accessed on 13/03/2020).
22. 'Baking Point: George Borwick & Sons'. *Let's Look Again*, 2016 http://letslookagain.com/tag/history-of-borwicks-baking-powder/ (Accessed on 13/03/2020
23. British Newspaper Library, *Reading Evening Post* (Tuesday 15 February 1966)
24. British Newspaper Library, *Manchester Evening News* (Friday 23 August 1946)
25. 'About Us', *Hollands Pies*, http://www.hollandspies.co.uk/about-us/our-story/ (Accessed on 16 /03/2020)
26. MacEwan, P., *Pharmaceutical Formulas* (The Chemist and Druggist, London, 1914), p.308
27. Hallam, J., *To Grandma with Love* (Souvenir Press, London, 1981), p.171
28. Timmins, G., *Made in Lancashire: A History of Regional Industrialisation* (Manchester University Press, 1988), p.201
29. British Newspaper Library, *Lancashire Evening Post* (Monday 6 May 1957)
30. 'J.Lyons & Co. Symbol Biscuits', https://www.kzwp.com/lyons1/symbol.htm (Accessed 10/03/2020)
31. British Newspaper Library, *Burnley Express* (Wednesday 6 March 1907)
32. Axon, E. (ed.), *Bygone Lancashire* (W., Andrews and Co., Hull, 1892), p.172
33. *The Bee, fire-side companion and evening tales* (Henry Fisher, London, 1820), p.221
34. Raffald, E., *The Experienced English Housekeeper* (Davies and Booth, Leeds, 1818), p.160
35. 'Life in East Lancashire', *The Historic Society of Lancashire and Cheshire*, p.108, https://www.hslc.org.uk/wp-content/uploads/2017/05/120-7-Brigg.pdf (Accessed 15/03/2020)
36. 'Vimto History', *Vimto*, https://www.vimto.co.uk/history.aspx (Accessed 17/03/2020)

37. Marsh, T., *Walking on the West Pennine Moors* (Cicerone, Krakow, 2012)
38. British Newspaper Library, *Blackburn Standard* (Saturday 21 January 1888)
39. British Newspaper Library, *Barnoldswick & Earby Times* (Friday 14 July 1950)

4. FAITIN AND THE FUTURE

1. Thompson, T., *Lancashire Lustre* (George Allen & Unwin, 1937), p.63-64
2. British Newspaper Library, *Liverpool Echo* (Tuesday 08 December)
3. 'Story of Margaret McColl (now Bate)', *BBC WW2 People's War: An Archive of World War Two Memories*, https://www.bbc.co.uk/history/ww2peopleswar/stories/39/a4067039.shtml (Accessed 05/03/2020)
4. 'Mrs Shirley Margaret Smith', *BBC WW2 People's War: An Archive of World War Two Memories*, 2005 https://www.bbc.co.uk/history/ww2peopleswar/stories/99/a4015199.shtml (Accessed 05/03/2020)
5. 'Mr C. L Tweedale' *BBC WW2 People's War: An Archive of World War Two Memories* https://www.bbc.co.uk/history/ww2peopleswar/stories/00/a4051900.shtml (Accessed 05/03/2020)
6. p.85 The Freckleton, England, Air Disaster, James R. Hedtke, 2014, McFarland, USA
7. *Story from George Fisher, 2004 WW2 People's War.* https://www.bbc.co.uk/history/ww2peopleswar/stories/60/a2963360.shtml
8. Hedtke, J. R., *The Freckleton, England, Air Disaster* (McFarland, USA, 2014), p.93
9. British Newspaper Library, *Market Harborough Advertiser and Midland Mail* (Friday 16 October 1942)
10. Walker, H., *Disappearing Foods: Studies in Foods and Dishes at Risk* (Prospect Books, Totnes, 1994) p.193
11. British Newspaper Library, *Rochdale Observer* (Wednesday 28 August 1940)

Bibliography

Abram, A., *A History of Blackburn: Town and Parish* (Heritage Publications, 2014)

Andrews, C., *The Country Cooking of Ireland* (Chronicle Books, California, 2009)

Anon., *The Old Established Eccles cake-maker, never removed, nor never will do, in The Bee, fire-side companion and evening tales* (Henry Fisher, London, 1820)

Axon, E. (ed.), *Bygone Lancashire* (W., Andrews and Co., Hull, 1892)

Axon, E., *Sunday in Lancashire and Cheshire* (1881)

Barton, B. T., *The County of Lancaster* (Wardleworth, Bury, 1874)

Bradley, R., *The Country Housewife and Lady's Director in the Management of a House, and the Delights and Profits of a Farm* (Browne and T. Woodman, London, 1732)

Carrick, J. C., *Wycliffe and the Lollards* (C. Scribner's & Sons, New York, 1908)

Carter, G, G., *Red Charger: A Trip on the Arctic Fishing Grounds* (Constable, 1950)

Chaucer, G., *The Miller's Prologue and Tale* (Cambridge University Press, Cambridge, 2016)

Clayton., *The Lancashire Witch Conspiracy: Histories and New Discoveries of the Pendle Witch Trials* (Barrowford Press, 2007)

Fowler, A., *Lancashire Cotton Operatives and Work, 1900-1950: A Social History of Lancashire Cotton Operatives in the Twentieth Century* (Routledge, Oxford, 2018)

Hallam, J., *To Grandma with Love* (Souvenir Press, London, 1981)

Harland, J., Wilkinson, T. T., *Lancashire Folklore* (Kessinger Publishing, 2003)

Harland, J., Wilkinson, T.T., *Lancashire Legends, Traditions, Pageants, Sports, &c.* (Routledge, London and Manchester, 1873)

Hartley, D., *Food in England: A Complete Guide to the Food that Makes Us Who We Are* (Piatkus, 2009)

Hedtke, J. R., *The Freckleton, England, Air Disaster* (McFarland, USA, 2014)

Hughes, G., *The Lost Foods of England* (Denver House, Derbyshire, 2017)

Humphrey Marshall, W., *A Review of the Reports to the Board of Agriculture, from the Northern Dept* (Thomas Wilson and Son, London, 1808)

Iredale, D.A., *The Rise and Fall of The Marshalls of Northwich 1720-1917* (1966)

Landless, V., *Preesall Salt Mines*, British Mining No. 11 (Northern Mine Research Society, 1979)

MacDonell, A., (ed.), *The Closet of Sir Kenelm Digby Knight Opened*, (Philip Lee Warner, London, 1669, 1910)

Partington, S. W., *The Danes in Lancashire and Yorkshire* (Sherratt & Hughes, London and Manchester, 1909)

MacEwan, P., *Pharmaceutical Formulas* (The Chemist and Druggist, London, 1914)

Marsh, T., *Walking on the West Pennine Moors* (Cicerone, Krakow, 2012)

May, R., *The Accomplisht Cook* (1660)

Miller, Gary, *External Influences on English: From Its Beginnings to the Renaissance* (Oxford University Press, Oxford, 2012)

Millers, N., *The Lancashire Nobby* (Amberley, Gloucestershire, 2009)

Morris, R. (ed.), *Liber Cure Cocorum* (A. Asher & Co. Berlin, 1862)

Nodal, J., H., Milner, G., *A Glossary of Lancashire Dialect* (Alexander Ireland & Co., Manchester and London, 1875)

Poole, R. (ed.) *The Lancashire Witches: Histories and Stories* (Manchester University Press, Manchester and New York, 2002)

Raffald, E., *The Experienced English Housekeeper* (Davies and Booth, Leeds, 1818)

Roud, S., *The English Year* (Penguin, London, 2006)

Stout, W., *Autobiography of William Stout, of Lancaster, wholesale and retail grocer and ironmonger, a member of the society of friends. A.D 1665-1752* (Simpkin & Marshall, London,1851)

The condition and treatment of the children employed in the mines and collieries of the United Kingdom 1842. Commissioners for inquiring into the employment and condition of children in mines and manufactories (William Strange, London)

The Folk-Song Society, in *Local Gleanings Relating to Lancashire and Cheshire: Volume.1-2* (London, 1875–78)

Thompson, G., *The Complete Practical Pastry Cook* (1889)

Thompson, T., *Lancashire Lustre* (George Allen & Unwin, 1937)

Timmins, G., *Made in Lancashire: A History of Regional Industrialisation* (Manchester University Press, 1988)

Tongue, M., *The Lancashire Witches: 1612 and 1634 Historical Society of Lancashire and Cheshire*, Volume 83 (1931)

Turner, J., *The Freckleton Tragedy, 1944* (Landy, Blackpool, 2007)

Walker, H., *Disappearing Foods: Studies in Foods and Dishes at Risk* (Oxford Symposium, 1995)

Waugh, E., *Home-life of the Lancashire Factory Folk During the Cotton Famine* (Manchester Examiner and Times, Manchester, 1862)

Webb, A., *Food Britannia* (Random House, London, 2012)

Woolley, H., *The Queen-like Closet; or, Rich cabinet stored with all manner of rare receipts for preserving, candying & cookery. Very pleasant and beneficial to all ingenious persons of the female sex* (1670)

ONLINE RESOURCES

An Archive of World War Two Memories www.bbc.co.uk/history/ww2peopleswar/stories

Proceedings of the Old Bailey online www.oldbaileyonline.org

The British Newspaper Archive www.britishnewspaperarchive.co.uk
The Historic Society of Lancashire and Cheshire www.hslc.org.uk
Uncle Joes Mint balls www.uncle-joes.com
Vimto History www.vimto.co.uk/history
Wellcome Archives www.wellcomelibrary.org

Acknowledgements

Lancashire has been my second home for some thirteen-odd years since meeting my husband, born and bred in the county. The warmth of the communities and the stunning contrasting landscapes, from rolling hills to breathtaking coastlines, chocolate-box villages and historic industrial towns, makes Lancashire both unique and very special.

I would like to thank the lovely folk of Freckleton, from where my husband hails and most of his family still live. In particular, huge gratitude to my mother-in-law Anne Kay and her friends and colleagues in and outside of the Mothers' Union, for providing recipes and little snippets of tasty information. And to Freckleton Library for looking after me so well during one of my recent talks and for inviting me back to speak again as soon as this book is published. To Janet Banks I would like to say a big thank you for sharing your stories and letting us tour the grounds of your house.

Credit must also be given to my smashing husband for contributing his marvellous photographic skills again and to my little boy for always being so patient with me when I must work.

Finally, to all the staff and crew at Amberley Publishing for your continued support and interest in my work – thank you very much.